21世纪应用型精品规划教材·物流管理

物流实务英语(英汉双语)
(第2版)

王 睿 主编

清华大学出版社
北京

内 容 简 介

本书内容涵盖了物流系统中各环节的专业英语知识，具体包括物流及供应链、采购与订单管理、配送、包装、仓储、库存管理、运输、物流单证、物流信息技术等主题。本书内容前后衔接，形成一体，每部分均包括难度适中的案例导入、中英文对应的精读课文，并附词组和带有音标的单词解释，在相应章节还增加了商务信函。同时，每一章都配有相应的习题，其中话题讨论、英语对话、案例分析等栏目体现了专业英语用书的综合性与实用性特点。为了方便教学和学习，本书还配有电子课件，其中包括教学课件及课后习题参考答案。

本书可作为高等院校物流管理及相关专业学生的专业英语课程的教材，亦可作为物流行业培训的教材，还可供具有一定英语基础的物流专业人员自学使用。

本书封面贴有清华大学出版社防伪标签，无标签者不得销售。
版权所有，侵权必究。举报：010-62782989，beiqinquan@tup.tsinghua.edu.cn。

图书在版编目(CIP)数据

物流实务英语：汉、英/王睿主编. —2版. —北京：清华大学出版社，2020.11（2025.1重印）
21世纪应用型精品规划教材. 物流管理
ISBN 978-7-302-56147-7

Ⅰ. ①物… Ⅱ. ①王… Ⅲ. ①物流—英语—高等学校—教材—汉、英 Ⅳ. ①F25

中国版本图书馆 CIP 数据核字(2020)第 143501 号

责任编辑：桑任松
封面设计：刘孝琼
责任校对：王明明
责任印制：宋　林

出版发行：清华大学出版社
网　　址：https://www.tup.com.cn，https://www.wqxuetang.com
地　　址：北京清华大学学研大厦 A 座　　邮　编：100084
社 总 机：010-83470000　　邮　购：010-62786544
投稿与读者服务：010-62776969，c-service@tup.tsinghua.edu.cn
质量反馈：010-62772015，zhiliang@tup.tsinghua.edu.cn
课件下载：https://www.tup.com.cn，010-62791865

印 装 者：大厂回族自治县彩虹印刷有限公司
经　　销：全国新华书店
开　　本：185mm×230mm　　印　张：14　　字　数：337 千字
版　　次：2013 年 6 月第 1 版　　2020 年 11 月第 2 版　　印　次：2025 年 1 月第 5 次印刷
定　　价：39.80 元

产品编号：086982-01

第 2 版前言

《物流实务英语(英汉双语)》第一版于 2013 年出版至今已有 7 年,本书在使用过程中受到师生的好评和肯定,被评定为 21 世纪应用型精品规划教材。鉴于中国物流企业聚焦"一带一路",将国际化作为新的发展方向和我国物流与供应链教学改革和发展的需要,作者将本版教材在上版基础上进行了修订,对内容和形式进行了整合和完善。

本书作为高等院校物流工程、物流管理专业的专业英语教材,选材广泛,内容新颖,针对性强。本书内容涉及物流、供应链概况以及物流的相关基本活动,包含采购与订单管理、配送、包装、仓储、库存管理、运输、物流单证和物流信息技术等内容。

在编写本书的过程中,作者参考了大量的书籍、文献和论文等,选材均来自国外物流专业权威和近期出版的期刊、时新教材、报刊资料及以世界物流大公司的年度报告和业务资料为内容建立的语料,内容丰富,材料翔实,具有很强的时效性、实用性、广泛性、新颖性和时代性,在此作者对这些专家和学者表示深深的谢意。在教材编写及修订中,曲露勃老师协助整理文稿,在此表示衷心的感谢。

限于我们水平有限,教材可能存在部分疏漏与不足之处,书中如有不尽如人意之处,期盼同行专家、使用本教材的师生和读者批评、指正。

编　者

第1版前言

伴随着中国对外开放的深入和全球经济一体化的到来,中国企业的机遇与挑战也相伴而来。企业生存环境的变化要求我国物流从业人员及在校学生必须提升自己的英语学习能力,具备直接用英语获取相关专业知识的能力和水平,因此,本书兼顾专业性和实用性两大特点,目的是培养学生专业英语阅读能力及文献翻译的初步能力。

目前市场上的物流英语教材普遍都是理论性的内容,涉及案例分析的较少,涉及物流实际业务的更少。尽管理论性的内容可以培养学生阅读外文资料的能力,却未能锻炼学生在实际业务中用英语进行交流沟通的能力。鉴于此,我们编写了本书作为高等院校物流工程、物流管理专业的专业英语教材,力求做到选材广泛,内容新颖,针对性强。本书内容涉及物流、供应链概况以及物流的相关基本活动,包含采购与订单管理、配送、包装、仓储、库存管理、运输、物流单证和物流信息技术等内容。每部分均包括难度适中的案例导入和中英文对应的精读课文,并附词组和带有音标的单词解释;在相应章节还增加了商务信函部分以提高学生的实战技能;每一章都配有相应的习题,其中话题讨论、英语对话等栏目为师生互动搭建了交流平台;此外,知识链接和课后案例分析部分可供学生进一步提高阅读能力和扩展知识面。

在编写本书的过程中,作者参考了大量的书籍、文献和论文等,选材均来自国外物流专业权威和近期出版的期刊、时新教材、报刊资料及以世界物流大公司的年度报告和业务资料为内容建立的语料,内容丰富,材料翔实,具有很强的时效性、实用性、广泛性、新颖性和时代性,在此作者对这些专家和学者表示深深的谢意。

曲露勃老师对书稿进行了认真细致的修改,在此表示由衷的感谢和敬意。由于水平有限,书中如有不尽如人意之处,敬请读者批评指正。

编 者

目　　录

Chapter 1　Logistics　物流 1
Part 1　Definition of Logistics　物流的定义 4
Part 2　7R Theory of Logistics　物流"7R"理论 7
Part 3　Main Activities of Logistics System　物流系统的主要活动 8
Summary　本章小结 11
Exercises　习题 11

Chapter 2　Supply Chain　供应链 15
Part 1　Definition of Supply Chain　供应链的定义 20
Part 2　Vendor-Managed Inventory (VMI)　供应商管理库存 23
Part 3　Supply Chain Management　供应链管理 24
Summary　本章小结 27
Exercises　习题 27

Chapter 3　Procurement and Order Processing　采购与订单管理 31
Part 1　Introduction of Procurement　采购概述 35
Part 2　Procurement Process　采购流程 42
Part 3　Specimen Letters　信函范例 44
Summary　本章小结 46
Exercises　习题 46

Chapter 4　Distribution　配送 51
Part 1　Definition of Distribution　配送的定义 54
Part 2　Distribution Center　配送中心 55
Part 3　Distribution Process　配送流程 57
Summary　本章小结 60
Exercises　习题 60

Chapter 5　Packaging　包装 65
Part 1　Introduction of Packaging　包装概述 68

  Part 2 Packing Materials 包装材料 ... 70
  Part 3 Packing Mark 包装标识 ... 73
  Part 4 Specimen Letters 信函范例 ... 76
 Summary 本章小结 ... 78
 Exercises 习题 ... 78

Chapter 6 Warehousing 仓储 ... 83
  Part 1 Introduction of Warehousing 仓储的概述 ... 86
  Part 2 Warehousing Layout 仓储规划 ... 88
  Part 3 Warehousing Operation Process 仓储运作流程 ... 91
  Part 4 Specimen Letters 信函范例 ... 94
 Summary 本章小结 ... 95
 Exercises 习题 ... 95

Chapter 7 Inventory Management 库存管理 ... 99
  Part 1 Definition of Inventory Management 库存管理的定义 ... 102
  Part 2 ABC Classification ABC 分类 ... 105
  Part 3 Collaborative Inventory Replenishment 联合库存补充 ... 108
 Summary 本章小结 ... 111
 Exercises 习题 ... 111

Chapter 8 Transportation 运输 ... 115
  Part 1 Definition of Transportation 运输的定义 ... 118
  Part 2 Transport Functionality and Principles 运输的作用和原则 ... 121
  Part 3 Intermodal Transportation 多式联运 ... 124
  Part 4 Specimen Letters 信函范例 ... 129
 Summary 本章小结 ... 130
 Exercises 习题 ... 131

Chapter 9 Logistics Documents 物流单证 ... 135
  Part 1 Documents in Logistics 物流单据 ... 137
  Part 2 Letter of Credit 信用证 ... 149
 Summary 本章小结 ... 154
 Exercises 习题 ... 154

Chapter 10　Logistics Information Technology　物流信息技术 157

　　Part 1　Definition of LIS 物流信息系统的定义 160
　　Part 2　Barcode and Scanning Technologies 条形码及扫描技术 161
　　Part 3　Radio-Frequency Exchange Technology 无线射频交换技术 165
　Summary 本章小结 168
　Exercises 习题 168

Appendix: Logistics Vocabularies　物流词汇 171

References　参考文献 211

Chapter 1

Logistics
物流

How a Bottle of Coca-Cola (coke) Moves to an End Consumer?
一瓶可口可乐是如何到达终端消费者手中的？

If a consumer wants to have a bottle of Coca-Cola (Coke), he can choose to

A. go straight to the **manufacturer**, buy it at **ex-factory price** (e.g. 1.50 Yuan/bottle) but pay extra costs for bus fare (e.g. 5 Yuan or more), totaling 6.50 Yuan plus time cost (hours of bus travel), or

B. go to a supermarket and buy it at retail price (e.g. 2.50 Yuan/bottle) with minimal time cost.

Choice A is rarely the case because the total logistics cost of direct purchase from the manufacturer is **prohibitive** for any individual (2.6 times as much as the **retail** price in the above case), though its purchase price is much lower than the retail price.

Choice B is most popular for individual consumers, in which the customer pays a higher retail price **in exchange for** ease of shopping and **exemption** of the **time-consuming** travel to the manufacturer, in addition to a lower total cost.

Generally speaking, movements of goods/products observe the typical supply chain model (See Figure 1-1).

manufacturer
[ˌmænjuˈfæktʃərə]
n. 制造商；[经] 厂商

ex-factory price
出厂价

prohibitive
[prəuˈhɪbɪtɪv]
adj. (费用、价格等)高得负担不起的

retail [ˈriːteɪl]
n. 零售

in exchange for
交换

exemption
[ɪɡˈzempʃən]
n. 免除，豁免；免税

time-consuming
[taɪmkənˌsjuːmɪŋ]
adj. 耗时的

如果客户想买一瓶可口可乐，他可能选择：

A.直接到厂家以出厂价(如1.50元/瓶)购买，但要支付额外的巴士费(如5元或更多)，总计6.50元，还要另加时间成本(数小时的巴士乘坐)，或者

B.去超市以零售价购买(如2.50元/瓶)，时间成本最低。

A 选择是极少出现的情况，因为从厂家直接购买的总物流成本对于个人而言是极其高的(在上述的情况中，达到了零售价的2.6倍)，虽然采购价要比零售价低得多。

B 选择是个人零散客户最常用的选择，在此种方式下，客户支付较高的零售价，在享有较低总成本的同时，还可以换取购物的轻松并免除到厂家取货的耗时旅程。

一般来说，商品/产品的流转需要遵循典型的供应链模式(见图1-1)。

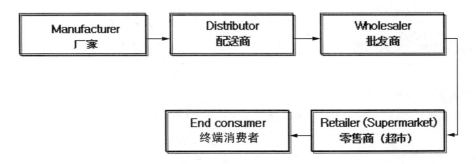

Figure 1-1　A Typical Supply Chain

图 1-1　典型的供应链

The Coca-Cola soft drink product moves by the typical supply chain. The retail price is higher because value is added to the product as it passes through each node in the supply chain (See Figure 1-2).

可口可乐软饮料的供应链就是依照典型的形式运转的，其零售价更高，是因为当产品经过供应链的每个节点时增加了价值（见图 1-2）。

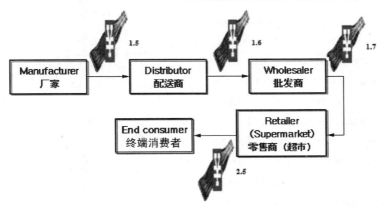

Figure 1-2　A Presumptive Value-added Model

图 1-2　推定增值模型

Learning Objectives 【学习目标】

- To learn the definition of logistics.
- To learn the 7R theory of logistics.

- To learn the activities in logistics system.

Key Terms 【关键词】

logistics	物流	transportation	运输
production planning	生产规划	inventory management	库存管理
packaging	包装	customer service	客户服务

Part 1　Definition of Logistics 物流的定义

1. Introduction of Logistics

"**Logistics**" is a term, which originates from both the army and French. According to the French, the Baron of Jomini, who was born in Swiss and had served in Napoleon's army before joining the Russian's and who later founded the Military Academy of St. Petersburg, first used the term in the early 19th century. So in a military sense, the term "logistics" **encompasses** transport organization, army **replenishments** and material maintenance.

In the business world, however, the concept of "logistics" was applied solely to "Material Replenishment Programs" (MRP) and was confined to the manufacturing sector at the beginning. Therefore, the extension of the concept to involve company operations is a relatively new one and the earliest usage dates back to the 1950s in the U.S.

CSCMP(Council of Supply Chain Management Professionals) has given an authoritative definition which is widely

logistics
[ləʊˈdʒɪstɪks]
n. [军] 后勤

encompass
[ɪnˈkʌmpəs]
vt. 包含；包围，环绕

replenishment
[rɪˈplenɪʃmənt]
n. 补充，补给

1. 物流简介

"物流"一词来源于军队和法语。该词于 19 世纪初被祖文尼男爵率先采用。祖文尼是一名原籍瑞士的军官，他在投奔沙皇俄国军队之前在拿破仑军中服役，之后一手创立"圣彼得堡军事学院"。就军事意义而言，"物流"一词意即运输编制、军队补给和物料保养。

然而，在商务界，"物流"的概念仅仅用于"物料需求计划"，并且最初只用于制造业部门。因此，该概念被扩展应用于公司是相对较新的，最早的使用始于20世纪50年代的美国。

美国供应链管理专业协会给出了一个权威的定义，该定义被物流专业人士广泛接受。"物流是供应链的一部分，它对产品、服务

accepted by the logistics professionals. "Logistics is a part of the supply chain process that plans, implements and controls the efficient, effective flow and storage of goods, services and related information from the point of origin to the point of **consumption** to meet customers' requirements."

consumption
[kən'sʌmpʃən]
n. 消费；消耗

和相关信息从原产地到消费地的高效率和高效力的流动及存储进行规划、实施和控制，以满足客户的要求。"

专栏 1-1　美国供应链管理专业协会(简称 CSCMP)

　　1963 年在美国成立的美国供应链管理专业协会——Council of Supply Chain Management Professionals——英文简称 CSCMP，原名物流管理协会(简称 CLM)，是物流和供应链管理领域最有影响力的个人参与的行业组织。CSCMP 凭借会员的积极参与和杰出才能，一直致力于推动物流业的发展，为物流从业人员提供教育机会和信息。为实现这一目标，物流协会向行业人士提供了种类繁多的项目、服务及相关活动，促进从业人员的参与，了解物流业，从而对物流事业作出贡献。

　　CSCMP 特别关注以下三个重要领域。

　　——通过行业内的交流和对话，创造机会，提高和发展物流管理水平。

　　——通过计划和指导研究来推动物流理论和实践的知识发展。

　　——作为一个资源宝库，使人们清楚地了解物流对商业活动的重要意义以及它在全球经济中的关键性地位。

　　美国供应链管理专业协会是全球性物流业的个人组织，拥有约 15000 名来自世界各地的会员，每年有超过 6000 名会员参加年会，这个事实表明，成为 CSCMP 的会员，其象征意义已远非表明在行业内拥有会员身份这样简单。

http://www.cscmpchina.org/

2. Other Definitions of Logistics

There are various definitions of different versions. The term is defined as follows.

- **Logistics(business definition):** Logistics is defined as a business planning **framework** for the management of material, service, information and capital flows. It includes the increasingly complex information, communication and control systems required in today's business environment.

　　—(Logistics Partners, Helsinki, FI, 1996)

- **Logistics(military definition):** Logistics is the science of planning and carrying out the movement and maintenance of forces. It is related to many aspects of **military** operations that deal with the design and development, **acquisition**, storage, movement, distribution, maintenance, evacuation and disposition or material; movement, **evacuation**, and hospitalization of personnel; acquisition of construction, maintenance, operation and disposition of facilities; and acquisition or furnishing of services.

　　—(JCS Pub 1-02 excerpt)

　　—Reference: *American Heritage Dictionary*

- **Logistics:** Logistics is the process of planning, implementing, and controlling the efficient, effective flow and storage

framework
['freɪmwɜːk]
n. 框架；构架；结构

military
['mɪlɪtəri]
adj. 军事的

acquisition
[ˌækwɪ'zɪʃən]
n. 获得；获得物；购置

evacuation
[ɪˌvækju'eɪʃən]
n. 疏散；撤离

2. 物流的其他定义

"物流"一词有不同版本的各种定义，具体如下。

- 物流(商业定义)：物流被定义为管理物流、服务流、信息流和资金流的商业计划的构架。它包括当今商业环境所需要的日益复杂的信息、通信和控制系统。

　　——(物流管理合伙人，赫尔辛基，芬兰，1996)

- 物流(军事定义)：物流是计划、执行军队的调动与维护等方面的一门科学。物流与军事活动的诸多方面有关，包括军事物资的设计、开发、采购、储存、运输、分配、保养、疏散及废料处置；军事人员的运输、疏散和医疗；军事装备的建设性采购、保养、运营及废物处理；军事服务的采购与提供。

　　——(参谋长联席会议 1-02 摘录)

　　——《美国传统字典》

- 物流：物流是对货物、服务及相关信息

of goods, services, and related information from the point of origin to the point of consumption for the purpose of **conforming** HT customer requirements. Note that this defini-tion includes inbound, outbound, internal, and external movements, and return of materials for environmental purposes.

—(Reference: Council of Logistics Management)

- **Logistics:** Logistics is the process of planning, implementing, and controlling the efficient, cost effective flow and storage of raw materials, in-process **inventory**, finished goods and related information from the point of origin to the point of consumption for the purpose of meeting customer requirements.

—(Reference: Canadian Association of Logistics Management)

conform to
符合；遵循

inventory
['ɪnvəntərɪ]
n. 存货；清单

从起源地到消费地的有效率、有效益的流动和储存进行计划、执行和控制，以满足顾客要求的过程。该过程包括流入、流出、内部和外部的移动及以保护环境为目的的物料回收。

——（参考：美国物流管理协会）

- **物流**：物流是对原材料、在制品库存、产成品及相关信息从起源地到消费地的有效率、有效益的流动和储存进行计划、执行和控制，以满足顾客要求的过程。

——（参考：加拿大物流管理协会）

Part 2　7R Theory of Logistics　物流"7R"理论

Logistics is sometimes described as achieving the "seven rights":
getting the right thing;
in the right quantity;
in the right quality;
to the right place;
at the right time;
in the right **condition**;
at the right price.

condition
[kən'dɪʃən]
n. 条件；情况

物流有时又被描述为达到"7个适当"：
获得适当的物品；
以适当的数量；
以适当的质量；
到达适当的地点；
在适当的时间；
以适当的状况；
以适当的价格。

In practice, logistics **refers to** the systematic management of the various activities required from the point of production to the customer. Getting the right amount of goods to the right place at the right time is critical, especially in an age when **budgets** are tight and customer demand is unpredictable.

In order to succeed in today's global marketplace, companies must be ever **cognizant** of these trends and develop a logistics management strategy that capitalizes on the best-of-breed technology solution available today, so that they can meet the demands of their customers today and be well prepared for the future.

refer to
参考；涉及；
指的是；适用于

budget
['bʌdʒɪt]
n. 预算

cognizant
['kɒgnɪzənt]
adj. 察知的

实际上，物流是指从生产地点到客户所需各种活动的系统管理。尤其是在资金预算紧张和客户需求无法预测时，在适当的地点和时间得到适当数量的货物显得颇为关键。

为了赢得全球市场，公司必须清楚地知道市场发展方向并制定相应的物流管理战略，要充分利用先进技术，这样才能更好地满足客户需求并为未来的发展做好充足的准备。

Part 3　Main Activities of Logistics System　物流系统的主要活动

To make a logistics system function, a variety of activities such as procurement, packaging, transportation, warehousing, inventory control, information processing, customer service must execute together. This is no small task, especially in an environment that is becoming increasingly demanding. Let's briefly introduce some of these main activities of logistics system.

● Procurement

Procurement refers to purchasing raw materials, **component** parts, and supplies from outside companies to support the organization operation. Since these inputs can have direct impact on both the cost and quality of the final

component
[kəm'pəunənt]
n. 成分；组件

一个物流系统要运作起来，需要各种活动的共同参与。这些活动包括采购、包装、运输、仓储、库存控制、信息处理、客户服务等。在市场环境变得越来越严苛的情况下，要完成这些任务并不简单。以下介绍物流系统中一些主要的活动。

● 采购

采购是指从公司外部购买原材料、零部件等以支持公司的运作。因为这些购入的物品对公司的成本和最终

product/service offered to the customer, this activity is important to the overall success of the logistics effort.

- Packaging

Packaging can have both marketing (consumer packaging) and logistical (industrial packaging) **dimensions**. Industrial packaging focuses on protecting the product while it is being shipped and stored. Too much packaging increases costs while **inadequate** protection can result in merchandise damage and, **ultimately**, customer dissatisfaction.

- Warehousing

Warehousing refers to places where inventory can be stored for a particular period of time. In the past decades, important changes have occurred **with respect to** the role of warehousing in contemporary logistics system.

- Inventory management

Inventory refers to stocks of goods that are maintained for a variety of purposes, such as for **resale** to others, as well as to support manufacturing or assembling processes. To achieve good inventory management, logisticians need to balance the cost of maintaining additional products on hand against the risk of not having those items when the customer wants them.

- Transportation

Transportation refers to the physical movement of goods from one point to another point. It involves selection of the transport mode, **route** of the shipment,

dimension
[dɪˈmenʃ(ə)n]
n. 规模，大小

inadequate
[ɪnˈædɪkwɪt]
adj. 不充分的，不适当的

ultimately
[ˈʌltɪmətlɪ]
adv. 最后

with respect to
关于；至于

resale
[ˈriːseɪl]
n. 转售；零售

route [ruːt]
n. 路线；途径

向顾客提供的产品或服务的质量有着直接影响，所以这一活动对物流的整体功能的实现起着很重要的作用。

- 包装

包装包括营销包装(消费包装)和物流包装(工业包装)两种类型。工业包装强调的是在商品运输和存储过程中所起的保护作用。包装过度会增加成本，但是缺少应有的保护会导致货物损坏，最终使客户不满。

- 仓储

仓储指的是一段时间内用来存储货物的地方。在过去的十年中，仓储在现代物流系统中的角色发生了重要的变化。

- 库存管理

库存指的是为不同目的而保留的储存货物，例如要转卖给他人的货物、用于支持生产或组装过程的货物。良好的库存管理要求物流人员在保有现存的额外的产品所产生的成本和在顾客需要时缺货的风险之间取得平衡。

- 运输

运输指的是物品从一点向另一点的物理移动。运输包含选择运输方式和路线，在地方和国家规章制度范围内运营和选择承运人。运输

compliance with regulation in the region of the country, and selection of carriers. Transportation is often the most costly logistics activity, and can range from 40%~60% of a firm's total logistics cost.

● Information management

Information is what links all areas of the logistics system together. Since the development of IT technology resulted in price reduction of computers and software, founding an information system has become **affordable** even to small organizations. Indeed, firms are linking their internal logistics information systems with those of their suppliers, customers and other partners. Such an open exchange of information can result in faster order placement, quicker delivery, and greater accountability throughout the logistics process.

● Customer service

The ultimate purpose of any logistics system is to satisfy customers. Customer service policy might include the following:

An understanding of the different market segments that exist; an awareness of the customer's needs or perceived needs within this segmentation; the determination of clearly defined and quantifiable standards of customer service in relation to the different market segments; an understanding of the trade-off between the costs and levels of customer service; measurement of the service provided; and liaison with customers to ensure an understanding and appreciation of the service

compliance
[kəm'plaɪəns]
n. 顺从，服从

affordable
[ə'fɔ:dəbl]
adj. 负担得起的

通常是成本最高的物流活动，运输成本能占到企业物流总成本的40%~60%。

● 信息管理

信息将物流系统各个领域联系在一起。信息技术的发展使计算机和软件的价格下降，即使是一些小型企业也可以承担创建信息系统的费用。确实，企业正将它们的内部物流信息系统和它们的供应商、顾客以及合作伙伴的系统联系起来。这种对外信息交换缩短了下单、送货的时间，提高了整个物流流程的可靠性。

● 客户服务

任何物流系统的最终目的都是为了满足顾客的需要。客户服务策略包括：

理解不同的细分市场；具有在不同的细分市场里发掘客户需求的事项；对于不同的细分市场，确定清晰明确的可量化的客户服务标准；懂得在客户服务成本与水平之间进行权衡；衡量所提供的服务；联系客户以确保理解和正确评价所提供的服务。

在以上活动中，有的传统上在企业中就扮演着独立的角色(如采购、生产规划、信息处理)，而另一些则通常

provided.

Some of these activities **traditionally** have a well-defined stand-alone role within a company (procurement, production planning, information processing), while others generally have been more closely associated with logistics (transportation, warehousing, inventory management, packaging). What **ties** all these functions together is their ability to impact customer satisfaction, and this can be achieved through good customer service.

We should keep in mind that one logistics system does not **fit** all companies. The number of activities in a logistics system can vary from company to company.

To understand these activities better, we will analyze them in closer detail in the following chapters of this book.

traditionally
[trə'dɪʃənəlɪ]
adv. 传统上；习惯上

tie [taɪ]
v. 绑；联结

fit [fɪt]
vi. 符合，配合；适合

与物流有更紧密的关系(如运输、仓储、库存管理、包装)。这所有活动之所以能联系在一起，是因为它们都会对客户满意度产生影响，并最终通过好的客户服务这一活动得以实现。

同一套物流系统不能适用于所有的企业，这是我们必须要牢记的。各个公司之间的物流系统所包含的活动可能是不同的。

为了更好地理解这些物流活动，我们会在以后的章节中对它们进行更详细的分析。

Summary 本章小结

In this initial part, a number of logistics definitions have been introduced. The important elements of logistics have been described, and these will be expanded in the subsequent chapters of the book.

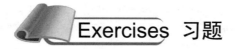

Questions for Review 复习题

1. What is logistics?
2. What does the term "logistics" originate from?
3. How do you comprehend the sentence "logistics encompasses much more than just the transport of goods"?

True or False 判断对错

1. There are a variety of definitions about the term "logistics", and each has slightly different meaning.

2. Logistics involves the flow and storage of "goods, services, and related information".

3. Logistics managers tend to maximize the number of handling whenever possible.

4. Exchange of information among different companies can result in faster order placement, quicker delivery, and greater accountability throughout the logistics process.

5. Good customer service is to make sure that the right person receives the right product with the right quantity at the right place, at the right time and in the right condition, even the cost is very high.

Topic for Discussion 讨论话题

Some people think logistical professionals should get a higher salary. Do you agree?

Logistics English Dialogue 物流英语对话

Introduction to a Logistics Company

(A, the sales representative of Zhongji Shipping Company, is talking with B, a potential customer.)

A: Welcome to our company, Mr. B. Nice to meet you.

B: Me too.

A: Mr. B, my name is A. Here is my card. I'm willing to introduce my company.

B: Thank you for a lot of care.

A: Our business covers import and export container transportation and agency, door-to-door pickup and delivery, customs clearance and warehousing.

B: I see.

A: Zhongji Shipping Company has become one of the market leaders in China's freight forwarding and logistics industry today.

B: Uh-huh.

A: We have helped Ford substantially reduce logistics costs.

B: Please explain it in detail.

A: Of course. That was one of the best results achieved at the beginning of the 2000s.

B: One of the best results? In what way?

A: We improved their management by optimizing their plans of demonstration before plunging into action. As a result, the overall utilization was raised considerably.

B: It's amazing.

A: If you are concerned about logistics questions, you can ask any one. We have a reputation for top service.

B: I hope so.

A: If you have a moment, I'm hoping to visit you.

B: Well, you are welcome. I'd like to hear your suggestion.

Case Study 案例分析题

Wal-Mart Wins with Logistics

Kmart and Wal-Mart were two retail merchandise chains that, a few years ago, looked alike, sold the same products, sought the same customers, and even had similar names. When the race began, people were quite familiar with the "big red K", whose stores dotted metropolitan areas, but few had heard of Wal-Mart, whose stores were in rural settings. Considering the similarity of the stores and their mission, analysts attribute the fates of the two chains primarily to different management philosophies.

In 1987, Kmart was far ahead, with twice as many stores and sales of $26 billion, compared to $16 billion for Wal-Mart. With its urban presence and a focus on advertising, Kmart had more visibility. In contrast, Wal-Mart began in stand-alone stores outside small towns, luring customers away from the stores in aging downtowns.

Kmart executives focused on marketing and merchandising, even using Hollywood star Jaclyn Smith to promote her clothing line. By contrast, Sam Walton, Wal-Mart's founder, was obsessed with operations. He invested millions of dollars in a company-wide computer system linking cash registers to headquarters, enabling him to quickly restock goods. He also invested heavily in trucks and modern distribution centers. Besides enhancing his control of the supply chain, these moves sharply reduced costs. While Kmart tried to improve its image and cultivate store loyalty, Wal-Mart kept lowering costs, betting that price would be proved more important than any other factor in attracting customers. Wal-Mart's incredibly sophisticated distribution, inventory, and scanner systems meant that customers almost never encountered depleted shelves or price-check delays.

Meanwhile, Kmart's mounted, as distribution horror stories abounded. Employees lacked the training and skill to plan and control inventory properly, and Kmart's cash registers often did not have up-to-date information and would scan items and enter incorrect prices. This led to a lawsuit in California, and Kmart settled for $985000 for overcharging its customers.

Over the year, it has been Wal-Mart's focus on logistical matters that enables it to keep its prices low and its customer happy and returning often. Today, Wal-Mart is nearly six times the size of Kmart.

Kmart continued its focus on ad circulars and promotional pricing into the 21st century, whereas Wal-Mart continued to focus more on supply chain efficiencies and less on advertising with the result that selling, administrative, and overhead costs were 17.3 percent for Wal-Mart and Kmart's were 22.7 percent. Wal-Mart was able to achieve prices that average 3.8 percent below Kmart's and even 3.2 percent below Target's. In 2002, Kmart went into bankruptcy and reorganization.

Discussion: Why does Logistics management improve organizations' efficiency and effectiveness in the 21st century?

Chapter 2

Supply Chain
供应链

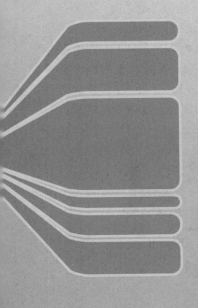

Case Study 案例导入

Beer Game

啤酒游戏

The Beer Game was originally invented by Jay Forrester at MIT Sloan School of Management in the early 1960s. It is a **simulation game** that can be used to demonstrate the benefits of information sharing, e-collaboration in the supply chain and a number of key **principles** of supply chain management.

Before a game begins, something must be known.

● Roles

(1) There are four roles in the game, as shown in Figure 2-1: retailer, **wholesaler**, distributor and manufacturer.

simulation game
模拟游戏；仿真游戏

principle
['prɪnsəpl]
n. 原理，原则；主义；本质

wholesaler
['həʊlˌseɪlə]
n. 批发商

啤酒游戏最初是由麻省理工学院斯隆管理学院杰伊·弗莱斯特教授在20世纪60年代初发明的。这个模拟游戏可以用来证明供应链中信息共享和电子协作的优势以及供应链管理的一些关键原则。

游戏开始之前，必须了解一些相关内容。

● 角色

(1) 在游戏中有四个角色：零售商、批发商、分销商和制造商，如图2-1所示。

Figure 2-1 Four Roles in Beer Game

图 2-1 啤酒游戏中的四个角色

(2) Each role from different companies is each other's customer or supplier in a

(2) 每个角色代表着不同的公司，它们在供应链中互

supply chain.

● Ground rules

(1) The game **extends over** a **fictitious** year and covers 52 rounds of one week each. You cannot take a break in the entire game.

(2) For the sake of simplicity, everyone sells only one product: Lover's Beer. One unit = One crate of beer.

(3) There are three costs involved in the game:
Inventory carrying costs = $1/case/week;
The **backlog** costs = $2/case/week;
Total cost = sum of costs at all four stages.

(4) The goal is to minimize total supply chain cost! You need to do all the **calculations**, and decide how much you will order each week.

(5) It takes two weeks for replenish-ment order to reach; shipment time is also two weeks.

(6) All demand is to be satisfied! If for some reason you cannot deliver, the product will be noted as backlog and you must deliver this order next time you have products in stock.

(7) NO **COMMUNICATION** AMONG STAGES! Retailers must not reveal actual customer orders!

(8) Players must not exchange any information other than that **constituted** by the order itself.

extend over
持续

fictitious
[fɪk'tɪʃəs]
adj. 虚构的；假想的；编造的

backlog
['bæklɒg]
n. [管理] 积压的工作；积压待办的事务

calculation
[ˌkælkju:'leɪʃən]
n. 计算，运算

communication
[kəˌmju:nɪ'keɪʃən]
n. 通讯；交流

constitute
['kɒnstɪtju:t]
vt. 组成，构成

为客户或供应商。

● 规则

(1) 游戏持续 1 年，每周 1 轮，一共需要 52 轮。整个游戏进行中不能停歇。

(2) 为了简便起见，每个角色只出售一种产品：情人啤酒，单位是箱。

(3) 游戏中有三种费用：
库存成本=1 美元/箱/周；
积压成本=2 美元/箱/周；
总成本=四个阶段的全部费用的总和。

(4) 目标是最大限度地减少整个供应链的成本！游戏参与者需要进行所有计算，并决定每周需要下的订单数量。

(5) 补给订单的送达需要两个星期；装运时间也是两个星期。

(6) 所有的要求都必须得到满足！如果由于某种原因游戏参与者不能运送产品，产品将标注为"积压"，并且当存货中再出现该产品的时候就必须运送这个订单。

(7) 游戏参与者在任何阶段都不可以相互交流！零售商绝对不可以透露实际的客户订单！

(8) 游戏参与者们不能交换除订单以外的任何信息。

- Course of the game

In each round, the following happens:

(1) Receive goods from the supplier;

(2) Receive orders from the customer;

(3) Deliver to the customer as ordered;

(4) Order new goods.

- Start the game

(1) Several games can take place at once, and several teams can therefore play against each other at the same time.

(2) One team orders four cases each week from the retailers in the first four weeks. From the 4th week on, the leader can order any quantity.

(3) The game will last 50 weeks, but can be concluded at any time.

- Overview

The results are shown in figures and diagrams when the game is over. Maybe most of the players feel **frustrated** because they are not getting the results they want. Feelings of confusion and disappointment are common. In the Beer Game, players enact a four-stage supply chain. Because communication and collaboration are not allowed among supply chain stages, players invariably create the so-called **bullwhip effect**.

The Beer Game is a role-play supply chain simulation that lets us experience typical supply chain problems. The purpose of the game is to meet customers' demands, through a multi-stage supply chain with minimal expenditure on back orders and

frustrated
[frʌ'streɪtɪd]
adj. 挫败的；懊丧的

bullwhip effect
牛鞭效应；长鞭效应

- 游戏程序

每一轮中，以下情况都会发生：

(1) 从供应商处接收货物；

(2) 从客户处接收订单；

(3) 按照订单向客户运送货物；

(4) 订购新的货物。

- 游戏开始

(1) 几组游戏可以同时开始，几支团队可以在同一时间内相互对阵。

(2) 团队在开始的前4周，每周向零售商订购4箱啤酒。从第4周往后，教师可以订购任意数量的啤酒。

(3) 游戏将持续50周，但可以在任何时间结束游戏。

- 综述

游戏结束后，将结果填写在图表上。大多数参与者会感到沮丧，因为他们没有得到他们想要的结果。感到困惑和失望是常见的。在啤酒游戏中，参与者们演绎了供应链的四个阶段。但是，由于供应链的各个阶段之间不允许通信和协作，参与者们总会制造所谓的牛鞭效应。

啤酒游戏是通过角色扮演模拟供应链，让我们体验供应链的典型问题。游戏的目的就是通过一个多阶段的供应

inventory.

- Discussing

Answer the following questions about supply chain, using the concepts you have learnt through the Beer Game.

(1) What went wrong? How can the performance be improved?

(2) What are the important factors affecting supply chain performance? What can be improved?

(3) How can IT help in improving supply chain performance?

链,以最少的开支满足订单、库存以及客户需求。

- 讨论

请利用你在啤酒游戏中领悟到的观念对供应链的问题作如下分析。

(1) (上下游之间)究竟出了什么错?如何增进(团队的)表现?

(2) 有哪些重要的因素影响了供应链的绩效?应如何改进?

(3) 如何应用信息科技提高供应链的绩效?

专栏 2-1　MIT

MIT 是麻省理工学院的缩写,麻省理工学院是世界上最好的理工学院之一。MIT Sloan School of Management 即麻省理工学院斯隆管理学院,其前身是麻省理工学院 1895 届的 Alfred P. Sloan(当时为通用汽车总裁)于 1952 年捐助 500 万美元建立的产业管理学院(School of Industrial Management),1964 年改名为斯隆管理学院(Alfred P. Sloan School of Management)以感谢出资赞助者。斯隆管理学院被认为是美国最好的商学院之一,在 2005 年被《美国新闻与世界报道》杂志评选为美国排名第四的商学院,仅次于哈佛商学院、斯坦福大学商学院和宾夕法尼亚大学沃顿商学院。

2012 年美国大学综合排名第五。

2011 年美国大学计算机工程专业(Computer Engineering)本科排名第一。

2011 年美国大学电气/电子/通信专业(Electrical/ Electronic/Communications)本科排名第一。

2011 年美国大学供应链管理/物流专业(Supply Chain Management/Logistics)本科排名第一。

MIT 官方网站:http://www.mit.edu/

Learning Objectives【学习目标】

- To learn the definition of supply chain.
- To learn the definition of Vendor-Managed Inventory (VMI).
- To learn the terms in supply chain management.

 Key Terms【关键词】

supply chain management	供应链管理	raw material	原材料
finished product	成品	material flow	物料流
upstream and downstream	上游和下游	information flow	信息流

Part 1 Definition of Supply Chain 供应链的定义

Figure 2-2 shows the major elements in a company's supply chain, in terms of those organizations with which it deals directly. The issues **associated with** the delivery of these products to the company **are referred to as** inbound logistics. After the company has added value by transforming the purchased goods and services, the finished products are then delivered to its distributors and/or customers. Similarly, the issues associated with the delivery of these products to the company's distributors and/or customers are referred to as outbound logistics.

(be) associated with
与……有关系；
与……相联系

be referred to as
被称为……

如图 2-2 所示，与企业直接交易的供应商构成企业供应链的主要成员。从供应商处采购直接供货到企业的配送事务，就称为内向物流。企业将采购的货物或服务等投入增值转换生产之后，最终的有形产品和无形服务被配送到分销商乃至最终客户手中。而产品从企业到分销商或客户手中的配送事务，就称为外向物流。

Chapter 2 Supply Chain
供应链

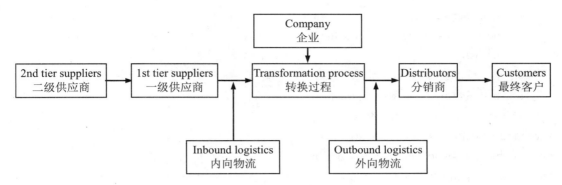

Figure 2-2 A Company's Supply Chain

图 2-2 企业的供应链

From a larger perspective, a supply chain can be defined as a group of organizations that perform the various processes that are required to make a finished product. Here the chain would begin with actual raw materials and end with finished products that are delivered to end users or final customers.

For example, if the finished product is a piece of **wood furniture**, then the supply chain, going **backwards** from the customer, will include the following:

- the retail operation where the furniture was purchased;
- the shipping company that delivered it;
- the furniture manufacturer;
- the hardware manufacturer;
- the **lumber** companies that harvested the wood from the forests.

If the end products are fresh fish fillets that are sold at a supermarket, then the supply chain will include the fllowing:

wood furniture
木制家具

backwards ['bækwədz]
adv. 倒退的；向后

lumber ['lʌmbə]
n. 木材

广义而言，供应链可以定义为：为有效地满足最终客户的需要，而由各个环节的成员连接成的一根链条。在这里，供应链从原材料开始，直至最终产品配送到最终客户或最终消费者手中。

举例来说，若最终产品是一件木制家具，那么供应链将从最下游的最终消费者往前追溯，包括：

- 为最终消费者提供木制家具的零售商；
- 运输公司；
- 木制家具制造商；
- 生产工具的提供商；
- 木材公司。

再如，若最终产品是超市中的鲜鱼片，那么其供应链包括：

- 超市；
- 送货的航运公司；

- the supermarket;
- the fresh fish supplier who delivered the fish;
- the fish processor who filleted them;
- the fishermen who caught them.

The structure of the supply chain can vary dramatically for different companies, even within the same industry. In addition, the role of an organization with respect to its span or degree of control over the supply chain can vary significantly. As an example, compare the supply chain for fish sold in a typical supermarket described above, with that of Spenger's, a long-established fish market and seafood restaurant located in Berkeley, **California.** Until recently, many of the various types of fish in its market and restaurant were caught on its own fishing boats and processed in its own operation. (Spenger's, founded in 1890, sold the last of its fishing boats in 1994 with the retirement of its owner and now buys fish either through brokers or from fishermen who work exclusively for Spenger's.)

As another illustration, Henry Ford, in order to support his huge River Rouge automobile plant just outside of Detroit, Michigan, invested heavily in iron ore mines, forests, **coal mines**, and even **cargo ships** that transported raw material on the Great Lakes. His goal was to gain total control over his supply chain (which, in the end, he realized was impossible). The greater the degree or span of control that a firm has with respect to its supply chain,

California
[ˌkælɪˈfɔːnjə]
n. 加利福尼亚(美国西海岸的一个州)

coal mine
煤矿

cargo ship
[水运] 货船

- 鲜鱼片加工商；
- 鲜鱼供应商即渔夫。

不同企业的供应链的结构差别很大，甚至对于同一个行业的不同企业也是如此。此外，企业对供应链广度和深度的控制差别也很大。例如，比较上述超市的鲜鱼片供应链与坐落在美国加利福尼亚州伯克利的历史悠久的施本格(Spenger's)海鲜馆的鲜鱼片供应链。以往施本格海鲜馆的各种鲜鱼都是由施本格的渔船自行捕捞并自行加工成鲜鱼片的，直到最近才有所改变。(施本格海鲜馆，创始于1890年，其经营者于1994年卖掉了最后一艘渔船，现在，它是从中间商或与海鲜馆有合作关系的渔夫那里采购鲜鱼)

再如，亨利·福特为了支持 River Rouge 大型汽车制造厂(设在密歇根州底特律)，曾经对铁矿、森林、煤矿甚至在航行于大湖(Great Lakes)上运输原材料的货船都投过巨资。他的目标是控制整个供应链(后来他意识到这是不可能的)。就供应链而言，控制得越深越广，纵向一体化程度就越高。换言之，与单纯制造和装配汽车的企业相比，福特汽车公司的运营是高度纵向一体化的。

the more vertically integrated it is said to be. In other words, Ford's operation could be described as being very vertically integrated in comparison to other automotive manufactures that focused **solely** on the manufacturing and assembly of the cars themselves.

Supply chain management, therefore, can be defined as the ability of a firm to work with its suppliers to provide high-quality materials and components that are competitively priced. The closeness of the relationship between the **vender** and customer, in many respects, differentiates due to different types of supply chain from another. The adoption of supply chain management **in lieu of** materials management or purchasing reflects top management's recognition of the strategic role of suppliers in contributing to the long-term success of the firm.

solely ['səʊlɪ]
adv. 单独地，唯一地

vender ['vendə]
n. 卖主；售卖者

in lieu of
代替

Part 2　Vendor-Managed Inventory (VMI) 供应商管理库存

Vendor-Managed Inventory (VMI) is a means of **optimizing** supply chain performance in which the manufacturer is responsible for maintaining the distributor's inventory levels. The manufacturer has access to the distributor's inventory data and is responsible for generating purchase orders.

Traditionally, customers (both retailers and final consumers) have been in charge

optimize ['ɒptɪmaɪz]
vt. 使最优化，使完善

of **monitoring** their own inventory levels and place purchase orders to vendors (retailer managed systems). In other words, the supplier only supplies the ordered goods while staying out of the retailer's inventory process. In this system the inventory level is usually high and thus incurs higher inventory-related costs.

However, as time goes by, retailers and business operators at large increasingly realize that there can be a better way to manage the inventories. That is, the inventory is **outsourced** to a third-party vendor (supplier) who is actively involved in the retailer's inventory process.

In recent years, there has been a growth in VMI. The vendor receives electronic data (usually via EDI or the Internet) that tells him the retailer's sales and stock levels. The vendor can view every item that the retailer carries as well as true **point-of-sale** data. The vendor **is responsible for** creating and maintaining the inventory plan. Under VMI, the vendor generates the order, not the retailer.

monitor
['mɒnɪtə]
vt. 监控

outsource
[aut'sɔːs]
vt. 把……外包
vi. 外包

point-of-sale
[,pɔɪntəv'seɪl]
adj. 销售点的

be responsible for
是……的缘由；
为……负责的

售商管理系统)。换言之，供应商仅仅提供所订购的商品，而置身于零售商的库存程序之外。在这一系统中，库存量通常较高并因此产生较高的库存关联成本。

然而，随着时间的推移，零售商以及一般的商业运营者逐渐意识到，可以有更好的方法来管理库存，即把库存外包给一个积极参与零售商库存程序的第三方卖方(供应商)。

近年来，VMI 的使用在逐渐增长。在 VMI 中，供应商(通常是通过 EDI 或互联网)接收电子数据，这些数据告诉供应商有关零售商的销售及库存量。供应商能够看到零售商所持有的每一件商品的数量以及真实的销售点数据。供应商负责制订并维护库存计划。在供应商管理库存模式下，订单是由供应商而不是由零售商产生的。

Part 3　Supply Chain Management　供应链管理

A supply chain as a whole process ranged from basic **commodities** to selling the final products to the end-customers to recycling used products. Materials flow from a basic commodity to the finished

commodity
[kə'mɒdɪtɪ]
n. 商品，货物；日用品

供应链涵盖了从基础商品(指原材料)到出售终端产品给终端客户再到回收旧产品的整个流程。物资从基础商品流向成品，产品使用后

product, and then the product is recycled after use. For instance, **aluminum ore** from a **bauxite** mine as a source of material flow is produced into a can of cola as the finished product. And then, the empty can is recycled. The analogy to water flow in a river is often used to describe organizations near the source as upstream, and those near the end-customers as downstream.

Alternatively, partnership can be formed among all the participants in the supply chain. There is a collective as well as an individual role to play in the conversion of commodities into finished products. At each stage of the conversion, there may be returns that may be reject material from the processing firm, or waste that needs to be recycled.

Supply chain management can be defined as "the systemic, strategic **coordination** of the traditional business functions and the tactics across these business functions within a particular company and across businesses in the supply chain, for the purposes of improving the long-term performance of the individual companies and the supply chain as a whole".

Each partner in a supply chain is responsible directly for a process that adds value to a product. The process may be referred to transforming inputs in the form of materials and information into outputs in the form of goods and services. In the case of the cola can, partners carry out processes

---

aluminum ore
[矿物] 铝矿

bauxite
['bɔːksaɪt]
n. 矾土，[矿物] 铁铝氧石；[矿物] 铝土矿

coordination
[kəʊˌɔːdɪ'neɪʃən]
n. 协调，调和；对等，同等

又得到回收。例如，来自铝土矿的铝金属作为物资流的源头被制成可乐罐子(成品)，而后空罐子又被回收。像流淌不息的河流，供应链中靠近生产源头的企业称为上游，靠近终端客户的企业称为下游。

换句话说，供应链中的所有参与者都可以形成伙伴关系。因为在商品转变为最终产品的过程中，企业不仅要发挥个体的作用还要发挥集体作用。在转变的每一个阶段，都可能有来自加工企业的次料回笼或者废料回收。

供应链管理可以定义如下："为了提高供应链上单个企业以及整条供应链的长期绩效，而对企业内以及供应链上企业之间的传统的商业功能和基于这些功能的经营策略进行的系统性的、战略性的协调。"

供应链中的每一个合作者都直接对产品增值的过程负责。该过程是指将物资和信息形式的投入转变为以商品和服务为形式的产出。以可乐罐子的制造为例，供应链中的合作者要经历采矿、

such as mining, transportation, **refining**, and **hot rolling**. The cola can have greater value than the bauxite (as per kilogram of aluminum).

Supply chain management involves planning and controlling all of the processes from raw material production to purchase by the end-user, and to recycling waste such as the used cans. Planning and controlling all of the processes links partners in a supply chain together in order to serve needs of the end-customers. In the commercial sector, serving customer's needs implies "more **competitive** advantages" and "greater value for money".

Materials and finished products only flow through a supply chain because of customer's behavior at the end of the chain. The focus of managing the supply chain as a whole is on integrating the processes of supply chain partners, of which the end customer is the key one.

The degree to which the end-customer is satisfied with the finished product depends **crucially** on the management of material flow and information flow along the supply chain. If delivery is late, or the product has bits missing, the whole supply chain will be at risk from competitors who can perform the logistics task better. Logistics is a vital enabler for supply chain management. Nearly half of supply chain costs are **incurred** instore, the other half is

refine [rɪ'faɪn]
vt. 精炼，提纯；改善

hot rolling
[机] 热轧

competitive [kəm'petɪtɪv]
adj. 竞争的；比赛的

crucially ['kruːʃəlɪ]
adv. 关键地；至关重要地

incur [ɪn'kɜː]
vt. 招致，引发

运输、冶炼和热轧的过程，从可乐罐中获得比铝土矿更多的价值(按所含每千克铝金属计算)。

供应链管理包含了从原料生产到终端用户购买再到回收废物(例如易拉罐)的整个过程的计划和控制，这种计划和控制把供应链中的合作者连接到一起，从而满足终端顾客的需要。在商业领域，满足顾客的需要就意味着"具备更多的竞争优势"和"产生更高的价值"。

原材料和最终产品因供应链终端的顾客需求而在供应链中流动。供应链的管理重点在于把供应链中以终端顾客为核心的各合作者的增值过程整合在一起。

终端客户对最终产品的满意程度关键取决于供应链中对实物流和信息流的管理。若交货出现延误，或者部分产品丢失，整个供应链将受到其他物流运作较好的竞争者的威胁。物流是成就供应链管理至关重要的因素。供应链中近一半的费用是储存货物时产生的，另一半则是协调整个供应链实

the logistics task of coordinating material flow and information flow across the supply chain.

物流和信息流的物流工作产生的。

Summary 本章小结

This chapter focuses on the concept of supply chain and supply chain management. Supply chain consists of firms collaborating to serve the needs of end-customers, to take advantage of strategic position and to improve operating efficiency.

Exercises 习题

Questions for Review 复习题

1. What is the supply chain?
2. What is VMI?
3. What is the significance of supply chain management?

True or False 判断对错

1. Supply chain consists of firms collaborating to take advantage of strategic position and to improve operating efficiency.
2. Supply chain would begin with actual raw materials and end with finished products that are delivered to end users or final customers.
3. Under VMI, the retailer generates the order, not the vendor.
4. Suppliers delivering these products to the firm are referred to as outbound logistics.
5. Supply chain operations require managerial processes that span functional areas within individual firms and link trading partners and customers across organization boundaries.

Logistics English Dialogue 物流英语对话

What Is a Supply Chain?

A: Please tell me what a supply chain is.

B: A supply chain is a complex logistics system in which raw materials are converted into finished products and then distributed to the final users.

A: What parties are involved in the supply chain?

B: A typical supply chain normally includes suppliers, manufacturers, distribution centers, warehouses and retail outlets.

A: Then what is the difference between logistics and the supply chain?

B: That's a big question. But first, logistics is part of the supply chain process, and...

A: ...and it focuses on the flow and storage of goods.

B: Exactly. A supply chain focuses on the whole distribution process, in which goods travel from suppliers through distributors to end users.

A: What is SCM(Supply Chain Management)?

B: SCM is to integrate, coordinate and control the flow of materials, information and finances in supply chains.

A: I hear there are two typical supply chain categories: the pull and push systems.

B: You are right.

A: What does MTO mean?

B: MTO stands for "make to order".

A: How does it work?

B: MTO means the manufacturer does not begin to make the product until it receives the order from the customer.

A: How about inventory?

B: MTO is an order-driven supply chain model and in this model the manufacturer does not hold inventories in usual cases.

A: Can I say MTS(Make to Stock)is the opposite of MTO?

B: You may well say so.

A: How does MTS work?

B: Production planners forecast and estimate the effective demand and inventories are held in warehouses and at the retailers.

A: That means MTS is a forecast-driven supply chain model.

B: Exactly.

Case Study 案例分析题

Supply Chain Management in Action in Dell Inc.

Excess inventory is like a leech that slowly sucks resources and money out of a business. To kill the creature, Dell Inc. is steadily replacing inventory with information. "Inventory is a security blanket," says Lance Van Hooser, director of e-commerce at Dell. The only reason why companies build up inventory is that they don't know about events that are going to happen. The more you know, the fewer inventories you will have to carry. Right now, Dell carries about seven days of finished product. The goal is to count the already-low-figure in minutes. The company is turning to the Internet to collaborate and conduct business with suppliers and customers at unprecedented levels.

Dell recently created customized Web pages for its top thirty suppliers, whose employees can log on to a secure, personalized site to view demand forecasts and other customer-sensitive information – such as who Dell's customers are and how much equipment each is ordering—to help them better gauge demand. As a result, suppliers can more easily match their production schedules to Dell's – making only what is needed, when it's needed.

Dell is also passing on data about its defect rates, engineering changes, and product enhancements for these suppliers. Since both Dell and its suppliers are in constant communication, the margin for error is reduced. Also, partners are now able to collaborate in real time on product designs and enhancements. Suppliers are also required to share sensitive information with Dell, such as their own quality problems. Van Hooser says it is easy to get its suppliers to follow Dell's lead because they also reap the benefits of faster cycle times, reduced inventory, and improved forecasts; and ultimately, the customer gets a higher-quality product at a lower price.

Dell is also using the Internet to create a community around its supply chain. The Web sites all have links to bulletin boards where partners from around the world can exchange information about their experiences with Dell and its supply chain. "The Internet is the core of everything we are doing," says Kevin Rollins, vice chairman of Dell." It provides the capacity to improve the flow of information, eliminate paper-based functions, and link global organizations."

Dell is also using the Internet to form tighter links with customers. For many of its business users, the company has created Web pages containing approved configurations, renegotiated prices, and new work-flow capabilities, so when an employee requests a new computer, the order is automatically routed to the appropriate person within the buying organization for approval. Rollins says Ford Motor Company saved about $2 million in initial procurement costs by using its customized Web page. "With information technology, the value of inventory is quickly being replaced by the value of information," he says.

Discussion: How can supply chain management improve organizations' efficiency and effectiveness in the 21st century?

Chapter 3
Procurement and Order Processing
采购与订单管理

AESCO's Order Processing Model
AESCO 公司的订单处理模式

The following sequence of operations took place every time a customer placed an order. Customers usually phoned in their orders, though some would mail or fax in **fresh** orders. The sales department received the order, and a salesperson would check if the customer had done business with AESCO in the past. With a first-time customer, a new customer account would be set up after a **credit** check by the accounting department. The next step would be to record the order details, **simultaneously** noting the importance of the customer to AESCO, and whether the order required assembly or special handling.

The salesperson would check his or her "stock screen", i.e. a computer screen that listed inventory, past **purchases** and purchase price for all materials carried by AESCO, to see if the requested material was available in the company's $2 million inventory. For those materials not in AESCO's inventory, the salesperson could dial into the manufacturer's computer and check the inventory position there. These "dial-up" links were available to most manufacturers.

fresh [freʃ]
adj. 新的

credit ['kredɪt]
n. 信用，信誉

simultaneously [ˌsaɪməl'teɪnɪəslɪ]
adv. 同时地

purchase ['pɜːtʃəs]
n. 所购物；获得物；购买

每当客户下了订单，就会启动下面的流程。尽管一些客户会用电子邮件或传真，但通常还是打电话下订单。销售部门的业务人员接到订单后，会核对该客户过去是否与本公司做过生意。对于新客户，会计部门会在核查信用后建立一个新的客户账户，接着记录订单细节，同时标出这个客户对公司的重要性以及这份订单是否需要组合或特别处理。

接下来业务人员会核对他/她的"库存显示屏"，判断客户需要的原材料是否能在公司价值200万美元的库存里找到。这个"库存显示屏"是一个列出了库存、以往的采购量和采购价格等资料的信息库。对于那些不在公司仓库库存里的原材料，业务人员会链接到制造商的电脑以找到该原材料的库存位置。这种"一键"链接可以联系到大多数制造商。

The salesperson priced the product based on AESCO's purchase price and the importance of the customer. **Margins** varied from 15% to 30% depending on the type of the customer and order size; the sales department had guidelines on the **appropriate** markup but discretion on the exact amount. Then, the salesperson would call the customer back with a price and delivery **quote**.

Once the order was finalized, the **delivery schedule** and payment terms were set up and the inventory position was modified to reflect the new order. The delivery schedule was then transmitted to the shipping department.

Getting back quickly to customer enquiries was **critical** to expanding business. Most industrial buyers were squeezed for time and wanted to spend less time generating purchase orders and **soliciting** multiple bids from vendors. Buyers at most companies are looking for someone who will turn their work around quickly. They are not necessarily looking for the lowest price.

AESCO usually was unable to fill a customer's entire order from inventory. Most customers expected immediate delivery of only a small part of their order, provided the rest of their request could be confirmed and scheduled right away. Thus, AESCO carried inventory only to satisfy those **portions** of the order that were needed

margin ['mɑːdʒɪn]
n. 利润；（期权）保证金

appropriate [ə'prəʊprɪeɪt]
adj. 适当的

quote [kwəʊt]
n. 报价

delivery schedule [贸易] 交货时间表

critical ['krɪtɪkəl]
adj. 决定性的，关键性的

solicit [sə'lɪsɪt]
v. 征求；恳求

portion ['pɔːʃən, 'pəʊ-]
n. 部分

业务人员根据公司的采购价格和客户的重要程度制定原材料的价格。根据客户类型和订单大小的不同，销售部门有一个恰当的加价原则并在加价的具体数额上非常慎重，通常将利润控制在15%～30%。之后，业务员会给客户回电告知价格和运费。

一旦订单得到最终确认，业务人员会确定发货时间和付款条款，同时修改库存反映新的订单。然后，发货时间表会被传送到运输部门。

迅速回应客户需求是扩展业务的关键。大多数工业客户都时间紧迫，他们要求花尽可能少的时间来确认订单并得到不同卖方的报价。多数公司都会寻找能迅速回复的供应商，他们并不需要寻找最低报价的供应商。

通常AESCO也不能从库存里完成客户的全部订单，多数客户希望能立刻运送订单的一部分，同时剩余部分能得到确认并确定发运时间。这样，AESCO只需要保持一定的库存来满足订单中被急切需要的部分。

immediately.

Because of limited inventory, AESCO had to **anticipate** customer's orders. "Our skill comes from reading the customer's mind," said a manager. AESCO kept very detailed records of customers' usage history, which enabled them to predict customers' demand. It relied on **sophisticated** computer models to predict demand, but this was a challenging task given by the product variety dealt with; e.g. a **catalog** from a single **capacitor** manufacturer might run into hundreds of pages with a range of different models. Investment in computers and technology amounted 1% of sales, and would be continuously increased.

anticipate
[æn'tɪsɪpeɪt]
vt. 预期，期望

sophisticated
[sə'fɪstɪkeɪtɪd]
adj. 复杂的

catalog
['kætəlɒg]
n. 目录

capacitor
[kə'pæsɪtə]
n. 电容器

因为库存有限，所以AESCO公司必须预测客户的需求，一位经理说："我们的技能是能读懂客户的想法。"AESCO公司保存了客户很详细的历史记录，这就使公司能预测客户的需求。预测需求依赖于复杂的计算机模型，因为要处理众多的产品种类，这是一个颇具挑战性的任务。例如，一个单一的电容器生产商可能会有成百上千页不同型号产品的目录。所以公司在计算机和信息技术方面的投资占到了销售额的1%，而且这方面的投资还会继续增加。

 Learning Objectives 【学习目标】

- To understand the definition of procurement.
- To learn the objectives of procurement.
- To analyze the process of procurement.

 Key Terms 【关键词】

procurement	采购	supplier	供应商
order processing	订单管理	delivery point	交货地点
subcontractor	转包商	vendor	卖主

Chapter 3 Procurement and Order Processing
采购与订单管理

Part 1　Introduction of Procurement　采购概述

1. Definition

Procurement is the acquisition of goods and/or services at the best possible total cost of ownership, in the right quality and quantity, at the right time, in the right place and from the right source for the direct benefit or use of **corporations**, individuals, or even governments, generally via a contract. Simple procurement may involve nothing more than repeated purchasing. Complex procurement could involve finding long term partners that might fundamentally commit one organization to another. Procurement is one of the essential links in the supply chain and as such can have a significant influence on the overall success of the organization. So over the years, many organizations have developed large departments to deal with the **sheer** weight of supplier **transaction**. In the past, the emphasis was to procure the goods at minimum cost with less attention paid to quality and timing, however, experience has shown that this was not the best course of action. The savings realized on minimum cost procurement have not been worth the cost of customer dissatisfaction due to quality problem. Today, quality, delivery and cost are quite properly treated with equal importance.

corporation
[ˌkɔːpəˈreɪʃən]
n. 公司，企业

sheer [ʃɪə]
adj. 完全的，彻底的

transaction
[trænˈzækʃən]
n. 交易

1. 定义

采购是指在尽可能少的成本消耗前提下，在适当的时间、地点，从适当的产地和供应商，以合同方式，为企业、个人或者政府获取适宜质量和数量的物料或服务的一种行为。简单的采购只是重复的购买行为。复杂的采购则还包括寻找从根本上效力于企业的长期伙伴。采购是供应链中至关重要的环节之一，因此它能够对整个组织的成功产生重要的影响。所以，近年来许多企业已经成立了很大的部门来专门处理与供应商的交易事宜。过去企业的重点在于追求尽可能小的成本开支，很少关注品质和时效性。然而，实践已经表明，这不是采购行为的最佳行动方针。在追求最低成本的过程中，因缩减成本而忽视质量，导致客户不满是不值得的。现今，质量、发货以及成本已被视为同等重要。

2. Procurement Objectives

- Ensuring the supply of raw materials

Clearly, without an assured flow of raw materials into a manufacturing plant, serious problems will ensue. These could take the form of plant **stoppages**, which will be enormously expensive. If expensive plant, machinery and labor are standing **idle,** then costs may be incurred at an alarming rate. Not only will cost be incurred, but also customers may be let down as goods are not available for delivery at the appropriate time.

With this in mind, procurement management can adopt several policies to ensure that supplies are always in the right place at the right time.

(1) The manufacturer could purchase the supplying company. This used to be common in **vertically** integrated organizations.

(2) Sufficient **safety stocks** may be held at the manufacturing plant to cover such **eventualities**. These stocks would be attractive carrying costs, but the alternative may justify this investment.

(3) The manufacturer may insist on the co-location of the supplier next to or close to the part itself.

(4) Where commodities such as **wheat** or **crude oil** are concerned, then options to buy certain quantities may be negotiated in advance.

---

stoppage ['stɒpɪdʒ]
n. 回合停顿；停止

idle ['aɪdl]
adj. 闲置的

vertically ['vɜːtɪkəlɪ]
adv. 垂直地

safety stock
[计] 安全库存，安全储备

eventuality [ɪˌventʃuˈælɪtɪ]
n. 可能性；可能发生的事；不测的事

wheat [hwiːt]
n. 小麦

crude oil
原油

---

2. 采购目标

- 确保原材料的供应

如果不能确保原材料流入制造车间，就会引起严重问题。这样会出现车间生产中断的情况，使得费用相当大。如果工厂、设备和劳动力都闲置，成本将会急剧上升。同时，由于成品货物不能在需要的时间运达而使顾客失望。

基于以上考虑，采购管理可以采取以下几条措施来确保供应时间和地点的准确性。

(1) 生产商购买供应商的公司，这在垂直一体化的模式中是很普遍的。

(2) 生产商保持足够的安全库存来应对意外事件的发生。这些库存会提示账面或持有成本，但是这种投资还是值得的。

(3) 生产商可以要求供应商的地理位置在自己附近。

(4) 当购买小麦或原油这类商品时，应事先协商购买数量。

Chapter 3 Procurement and Order Processing
采购与订单管理

- The quality of supplies

Ensuring that the goods and services purchased are of the right quality is important in that **substandard** supplies cause waste and a variety of problems:

(1) If the goods are unusable, then their presence will create a shortage in the required quantity, which in **JIT** environments may be crucial.

(2) Substandard goods will need to store awaiting collection. This could be a problem if the storage at the **receipt** stage is restricted.

(3) They will incur **transaction costs**, as the paperwork and time will be involved in rectifying the error.

(4) Substandard goods will undermine confidence in the supplier during the supply process.

Insisting on suppliers having quality management systems in place can help avoid these problems, as can **extrinsic audits** of suppliers premises. These audits may be carried out by the company's quality auditors. Supplier assessment programs will help highlight the main offenders.

- The price

This is the area that most people **associate** with during the purchasing process. The price will be dictated by certain factors.

(1) The negotiating skill of the purchasing team.

(2) The quality of the goods.

---

substandard [ˌsʌb'stændəd]
adj. 不合规格的；标准以下的

JIT (Just-In-Time) 准时制

receipt [rɪ'siːt]
n. 收到，收据

transaction costs 交易成本

extrinsic [ek'strɪnsɪk]
adj. 外在的；外来的；非固有的

audit ['ɔːdɪt]
n. 审计；经查核纠正的账目

associate [ə'səuʃɪeɪt]
常与with连用
v. 联合；与……联系在一起

- 供应质量

确保购买的产品和服务的质量是至关重要的，因为不合格的产品会产生浪费和一系列问题。例如：

(1) 如果有不可用产品的存在，那么将会使需求数量缩减，这在准时制(JIT)环境下是非常危险的。

(2) 不合格产品需要集中储存，如果在收货阶段不容许这种储存将会产生问题。

(3) 当涉及文书工作和时间来纠正这一错误时，将会产生交易成本。

(4) 在供应过程中，不合格产品有可能会削弱供应商的信任度。

对供应商实行质量管理可以避免以上问题。可以从公司挑选质量审核人员对供应商进行外部审核。评估机制有助于确认不合格的供应商。

- 价格

大多数人在采购阶段都会面临价格问题，价格由以下几个因素决定。

(1) 采购团队的谈判技巧。

(2) 货物质量。

(3) Detailed knowledge of the product being purchased. For example, when multiple retailers purchase commodities such as flour, they will have familiarized themselves with the costs of wheat and production before entering any negotiation.

(4) The relationship between the supply and the demand. In other words, if the product is **scarce**, then prices will tend to be higher as purchasers pay higher and higher prices for the goods. The opposite is true when the product is plentiful.

(5) The distance of the goods from their point of origin to the **delivery point**. Associated with this is the mode of transport used. The cost of transporting the raw materials may represent a large part of the purchase price.

(6) If the goods are being purchased by a buying group, then prices will be lower. A buying group is a number of companies grouped together in order to **pool** their buying power.

- The origin of the supplies

The origin of the raw materials may be critical. If the goods have to travel halfway around the globe, then not only will the transport costs be high but the lead time to delivery may be unacceptably long. It is also the case that not all parts of the world enjoy political stability. If supplies are interrupted for unspecified periods of time by political **strife**, then a company

scarce [skɛəs]
adj. 缺乏的，不足的；稀有的

delivery point
[贸易] 交货地点

pool [pu:l]
vt. 共用；合并；联营

strife [straɪf]
n. 冲突；争吵；争斗

(3) 商品的详细信息，例如当很多零售商购买面粉时，在谈判之前他们就已经对小麦及其生产成本非常熟悉了。

(4) 供求关系也会影响价格，也就是说如果产品稀缺，那么价格就会上涨，采购商将为此商品付出高价。如果产品非常多，情况就会相反。

(5) 产品从起始地到目的地的距离以及运输工具的使用种类会影响价格，运输原材料的成本在采购成本中将会占很大比重。

(6) 团购会使价格降低。所谓团购，是指很多公司通过联合采购来增强其购买力。

- 供应源

原材料供应地也很重要。如果产品要穿过半个地球才能到达，那么不仅会使运输成本提高，也会使运输期限无限延长。政治稳定性也会影响价格。如果政治纷争引起的意外动乱使供应商受阻，而公司又没有其他原材料供应商时，公司将会

could be in **dire** trouble in case it did not have an alternative source of raw materials. Important decisions must be made with these factors in mind.

● The method of supply

Smaller, more frequent deliveries typify a JIT system of supply. Inventory of raw materials may only be measured in hours and deliveries may even be made directly onto the production line itself. As more and more companies seek to reduce inventory costs, these types of arrangement have become more common.

Some companies look to suppliers to provide **vendor**-managed inventory. In this system, the supplier keeps and manages stocks of its product on the customer's premises. The customer only pays for the goods when they are used.

The process of receiving goods in a warehouse can be significantly speeded up, if suppliers provide the goods in the right quantities, at the allotted time, correctly labeled and **barcoded** where necessary. How the raw materials to be supplied needs to be determined and then discussed in advance with suppliers because they may not be able to meet the necessary **criteria**. It will be no good insisting on barcoded products if suppliers are unable to comply; and if a supplier can't comply, a buyer's receiving operation may be severely **compromised**.

dire ['daɪə]
adj. 可怕的；极糟的；极端的

vendor ['vendɔ:]
n. 卖主

barcode ['bɑ:kəud]
n. 条形码

criteria [kraɪ'tɪərɪə]
n. 标准，条件 (criterion的复数)

compromise ['kɒmprəmaɪz]
v. 妥协；使……陷入危险境地

陷入困境。在公司制定重大决策时需要考虑以上因素。

● 供应方式

小量的、交易频繁的运输一般采取 JIT 的供应方式，原材料的库存量变化频繁，每小时就会更新，产品甚至有可能直接从生产线调发，根本不会进库存。由于越来越多的公司在寻找降低库存成本的方法，这种方式将会得到普及。

有些公司希望实行供应商管理库存，即供应商保存和管理客户的库存。当客户用到此产品时再为此产品付费。

如果供应商在合适的时间，将正确数量的产品送达，且标签无误，在需要的时候进行编码，那么接货时间将会大幅度降低。买方应事先和供应商协商并决定如何运输原材料，因为这样供应商会查看满足必要标准的可能性。如果供应商不能履行商品编码，买方一再坚持是无益的。在这种情况下，买方对于收货条件可能需要做出巨大让步。

- The mode of transport used by suppliers

Many transport and delivery requirements need to be discussed prior to agreeing to deal with a supplier. In the past, company procurement managers have in some instances been **guilty of** making **spot** purchases of goods on the basis of price alone only to discover that the **consequential** cost of handling has been unreasonably high. Typical questions that need to be answered include:

(1) Will the goods be shipped by road, rail, sea or air?

(2) What sort of unitization is used?

(3) Will the goods be on pallets?

(4) What size are the pallets?

(5) Will the goods be **stuffed** inside containers and require considerable time and labor cost to unload?

(6) Should a transfer station be built to accommodate rail traffic?

- Make or buy?

The decision to make goods or provide a service as opposed to buying it in is one that is rarely straightforward. It is not always a simple question of cost. Other issues such as the company's **reputation** or production capacity may be included in the mix. The following is a list of the factors that often need considering:

(1) Cost. If the goods or services are to be provided **in-house**, then it is not simply the direct costs involved that need

guilty of
有过错；对……感到内疚

spot [spɒt]
n. 地点；当场；现场

consequential
[ˌkɒnsɪˈkwenʃəl]
adj. 间接的；结果的；重要的；随之发生的

stuffed [stʌft]
adj. 已经喂饱了的；塞满了的

reputation
[ˌrepjuˈteɪʃən]
n. 名声，名誉；声望

in-house
[ˈɪnˈhaʊs]
adv. 在内部地

- 供应商采用的运输方式

在和供应商签署协议时，应事先协商运输和交易要求。公司采购管理人员以前遇到过只注重压低价格，最终才发现总的运作成本异常高的例子。需要考虑的典型问题如下：

(1) 货物运输是采取公路运输、铁路运输、海运还是空运？

(2) 采取何种集装方式？

(3) 产品是否需要外包装？

(4) 包装规格是什么？

(5) 如果产品装在容器内，是否需要花费大量的时间和人力成本来拆卸包装？

(6) 是否需要设立转运站来接驳轨道交通？

- 采取自制还是外协

决定是自己生产还是外协并不容易，不仅要考虑成本问题，还要综合考虑公司信誉以及生产能力等一系列因素。以下是需要经常考虑的几个因素：

(1) 成本。如果产品或服务是内部交易，则不仅要考虑直接成本，还要考虑外延成本，比如投入资金的机会成本。也就是说，如果这

to be considered but the wider costs, such as the opportunity cost of the capital employed. In other words, could the capital tied up in this exercise produce a better return if invested in another activity? If the activity is to be provided by a supplier, then the costs associated with managing the supplier and the transaction costs should be included in the analysis.

(2) Ensuring supply. As mentioned above, if goods or services are not available when required, then significant extra costs may be incurred. The **reliability** of the supplier and the quality of its offering is another crucial part of the decision-making process.

(3) Production capacity. Some parts of an operation may be provided by **subcontractors** because a company does not have sufficient capacity within its operation to do the job itself. This may be a very sensible approach to take in certain circumstances. A vehicle fleet, for example, should be kept working full time. Therefore, it is better to have sufficient vehicles to achieve this end and subcontract any further work created by short-term increases in demand. Of course, the opposite is true in that if a production plant has spare capacity, then it may be correct to use it rather than have it stand **idle**.

(4) Competitive advantage. There may be certain products, components or processes that the company wishes to keep

reliability
[rɪˌlaɪəˈbɪlətɪ]
n. 可靠性

subcontractor
[ˌsʌbkənˈtræktə]
n. 转包商，次承包商；分承包方

idle [ˈaɪdl]
adj. 闲置的

笔资金投资在其他活动上是否收益更大？如果由供应商提供产品或服务，应该考虑供应商的管理成本以及交易成本。

(2) 确保供应。就像上面提到的，如果产品或服务在客户需要的时候不能按时提供，那么将会导致更大的额外成本。供应商的可靠性以及供应质量是决策过程中需要考虑的另一关键部分。

(3) 生产能力。对于一项作业，公司没有能力完全自己做时，某些部分就需要由其他公司来供应。在特定情形下，这是非常有效的方法。比如说，一支运输队，应该一直保持工作状态，因此，最好有足够的车辆来满足需求，并且当需求有短期额外增长时可雇用其他公司来做这些工作。当然，如果生产商有足够的能力就使用自己的车辆，而不是让其闲置。

(4) 竞争优势。毫无疑问，产品、零件及生产过程

secret and so it will not allow any other companies to gain information about them. A revolutionary new product may fit this situation.

需要保密以避免其他公司获知，开发新产品更是如此。

专栏 3-1　JIT

准时制生产

准时制生产方式(Just In Time，简称 JIT)，又称为无库存生产方式(stockless production)、零库存(zero inventory)、一个流(one-piece flow)或者超级市场生产方式(supermarket production)，是日本丰田汽车公司在20世纪60年代实行的一种生产方式。1973年以后，这种方式对丰田公司渡过第一次能源危机起到了突出的作用，后引起其他国家生产企业的重视，并逐渐在欧洲和美国的日资企业及当地企业中推行开来。现在这一方式与源自日本的其他生产、流通方式一起被西方企业称为"日本化模式"。

Part 2　Procurement Process 采购流程

The procurement process in modern business is a **cycle** consisting of seven steps.

现代商业中的采购流程是由一个循环的七个步骤组成。

cycle ['saɪkl]
n. 循环；周期

1. Information Gathering

If the potential customer does not already have an established relationship with sales/marketing functions of suppliers of needed products or services (P/S), it is necessary to search for suppliers who can satisfy the requirements.

1. 收集信息

如果潜在客户之前并没有和所需产品或服务的销售商/运营商建立关系，那么很有必要去寻找可以满足要求的供应商。

2. Supplier Contact

When one or more suitable suppliers have been identified, requests for **quotation** (RFQ), requests for proposals (RFP), requests for information (RFI) or

2. 与供应商联系

在确立一个或者几个合适的供应商之后，一般需要向对方提出报价请求(RFQ)、提案企划书(RFP)、

quotation [kwəʊ'teɪʃən]
n. [贸易] 报价单

requests for tender (RFT) may be advertised, or direct contact may be made with the suppliers.

3. Background Review

References for product/service quality are consulted, and any requirements for follow-up services including installation, maintenance, and **warranty** are investigated. Samples of the P/S being considered may be examined or trials undertaken.

4. Negotiation

Negotiations are **undertaken**. Price, availability, and customization possibilities are established. Delivery schedules are negotiated, and a contract to acquire the P/S is completed.

5. Fulfillment

Supplier preparation, expediting, shipment, delivery, and payment for the P/S are completed, based on contract terms. Installation and training may also be included.

6. Consumption, Maintenance, and Disposal

During this phase, the company evaluates the performance of the P/S and any accompanying service support, as they are consumed.

7. Renewal

When the P/S has been consumed

warranty
['wɒrəntɪ]
n. 保证；担保；授权；(正当)理由

undertake
[ˌʌndə'teɪk]
vt. 承担，保证；从事

renewal
[rɪ'njuːəl]
n. 更新，恢复；复兴；补充

信息请求(RFI)或投标请求(RFT)，或者直接与供应商取得联系。

3. 资质审核

必须咨询产品和服务质量证明，调查所有后续服务的要求，包括安装、维修和保修。必须检查所提及的产品或服务的样品，或者进行试用。

4. 谈判

进行谈判。确定价格、可用性以及定制的可能性。谈判内容包括交货进程，签订获取产品或服务的合同。

5. 执行

以合同条款为基础，供应商完成对产品或服务的准备、催交、装船、交货和支付，安装和培训也包括在内。

6. 消费、维护和处理

在这个阶段，公司对产品或服务的性能以及附带的服务支持等进行评价。

7. 更新

当产品或服务被消费或者处置而使合同终止，或

and/or disposed of, the contract **expires**, or when the P/S is to be re-ordered, the company reviews the quality of the P/S, determining whether to consider other suppliers or to continue with the same supplier.

expire
[ɪk'spaɪə]
vi. 期满；终止

者当产品或服务需要被重新订购时，公司对此产品或服务的质量进行评价，决定是否考虑其他供应商或者同该供应商继续合作。

Part 3　Specimen Letters　信函范例

1. Placing an Order

May 11, 2019

Dear Mr. Han,

Order of GC209 Wineglass

We have received our trial order for 50 units of the above wineglasses and find your products satisfactory. We therefore would like to place an order for 1000 units of the same model.

We agree to the price set as the last order, i.e. USD 8 each, CIF Singapore. Please accept this letter as our official order for the products, and deliver the order by June 15.

If the products are currently out of stock, we would appreciate that you send us catalogs of the alternatives. Thank you.

Yours sincerely,

Tianming Liu (Ms.)
Manager

1. 订购

韩先生：

订购 GC209 玻璃酒杯

早前试订的 50 件玻璃酒杯已收妥，产品品质理想，现续订 1000 件同一型号的酒杯。

本公司同意上次试购价，即每件 8 美元，价格为新加坡到岸价格，包括运费及保险费。请以本函作为该货品的正式订单，并安排货品于 6 月 15 日前装运。

若贵公司暂无存货，请寄上其他同类货品资料，以供参考比较。

经理

刘天明

2019 年 5 月 11 日

2. Confirmation of Order

May 12, 2019
Dear Ms. Liu,

Confirmation of Order (Order No. 12402)

We would like to confirm receipt of your order No. 12402. Thank you for ordering 1000 units of wineglasses from us.

The order is accepted subject to the general conditions stated in our offer of March 20. We would like you to provide us with the shipping instructions for our delivery arrangement.

You are most welcome to contact me if you have any enquiries about the order.

Yours sincerely,

Qiang Han (Mr.)
Manager

2.订货确认书

刘小姐：

订货确认书(订单编号：12402)

本公司日前收到贵公司的订单(编号：12402)，现确认订购玻璃酒杯1000件，感谢贵公司的订货。

本订单的确认基于本公司3月20日报价所注明的一般条件。请提供装运指示，以便尽早做出安排。

日后如查询该批订货，欢迎直接与本人联络。

经理

韩强
2019年5月12日

专栏 3-2 英文信函的基本特点

- 信头

日期写为：9(th) August, 2012/August 9(th), 2012；

如果是寄给特定某人的，通常写上 For the attention of/Attn 加上名字或者是收信人的职位，例如：For the attention of the Managing Director；

您的/我们的记录号通常写为：Your ref/Our ref (ref = reference)。

- 称呼

不知道收件人姓名写为：Dear Sir/Dear Madam；

知道收件人姓名写为：Dear Mr. Smith/Dear Mrs. Smith/Dear Ms. Smith；

(注意 Mrs.只能用来称呼已婚女性，而 Ms 不涉及婚姻状况和年龄)

收件人是公司的写为：Dear Sirs；

不知道收件人性别写为：Dear Sir or Madam；

多数时候，可以用名字直接称呼对方，例如 Dear Jim，这在英美国家是非常普遍的，但初次通信除外。称呼之后可用逗号，也可以不用标点，避免使用冒号(:)。

- 事由

为了提示信件的相关性，可以使用 reference 的缩写(Ref)。这一行跟在称呼之后，并用下画线标注出来，例如 Ref: Your Letter of June 1。

- 正文

正文如果很长，按意思分成自然段。

- 结尾

结尾由结束语和手写签名构成。

用 Sir、Sirs 和 Madam 称呼对方的，结束语用 Yours faithfully；

用姓氏来称呼对方的，结束语用 Yours sincerely；

用名字来称呼对方的，结束语用 Best wishes 或者 Regards；

如果开头称呼之后有逗号，那结束语之后也要加上逗号；

如果信件是你授权委托而写，那么在你的名字下面写上 pp (= per pro)加上委托人的名字。

- 附件

在信的最后，写上 Enc(s)/Encl(s)。如果有两个或者更多的附件，应该全部列出。

Summary 本章小结

This chapter provides an overview of procurement and the procurement process. It introduces the techniques and topics, and provides the methods used by procuring organizations to improve the procurement process in a competitive market. It also details the letters of procurement.

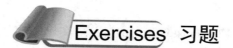

Exercises 习题

Questions for Review 复习题

1. What is procurement?

2. What are the steps of the procurement process?

3. What are the policies to ensure that supplies are always in the right place and at the right time in the procurement management?

True or False 判断对错

1. Procurement involves repeated purchasing.
2. Sufficient safety stocks may be held at the manufacturing plant.
3. The emphasis was to procure the goods at minimum cost with less attention paid to quality and timing.
4. Many transport and delivery requirements need to be discussed prior to agreeing to deal with a supplier.
5. If goods or services are not available when required, then few costs may be incurred.

Logistics English Dialogue 物流英语对话

(A, the purchasing officer in a university is talking with B, the marketing representative in an IT company.)

B: Good morning.

A: Hello.

B: We know that the university will build a new computer laboratory. Can you give me some details about that?

A: Yes. The project will need hundreds of computers, relevant softwares and accessories.

B: That's great. How do you do that?

A: Bidding. Companies should provide documents for initial evaluation, such as a copy of financial accounts for the previous three years, etc.

B: I see.

A: All responses will be fully evaluated according to the agreed criteria, including price, lead-time, quality and suitability of equipment, reputation of supplier, etc.

B: OK. That must include many documents and tables.

A: Yes. You can get that in our office, or download from our website.

B: Great. May I ask the payment terms?

A: Payment will be within 45 days of receipt of invoice and goods, but during this period installation and provision of training must be finished.

B: OK. When should we submit the tender document?

A: No later than 12:00 a.m. on July 21. And you may send it to the address on the invitation in a sealed envelope.

B: That will be no problem for us.

A: Please note that one printed copy of the tender document must be submitted, together with an electronic one.

B: All right.

A: You can provide companies or organizations, which have previously purchased the same equipment from you as a reference.

B: That is fine for us. We have sold the similar products to several universities in the past few years.

A: University contracts offer companies a marketing advantage, as those provide them a showcase to the students, who are potential buyers in the future.

B: That depends. It may or may not work.

A: Anyway, please consider this and the university looks forward to receiving a substantial educational discount.

B: OK. I will talk about this with my boss.

A: For more details, you can see the documents.

B: Thank you very much. We will work on it and submit it on time.

A: We look forward to seeing it soon. See you.

B: See you soon.

Case Study 案例分析题

Dell's Direct Model

Dell's direct model is based on direct sales from the PC manufacturer to the corporate customer or consumers. The model was driven by the "slicing" of the computer industry that took place in the mid-eighties. As Michael Dell explained, as a small start-up, Dell couldn't afford to create every piece of the value chain. We concluded we'd be better off-leveraging the investments others have made and focusing on delivering solutions and systems to the customers. If you've got a race with 20 players that are all vying to produce the fastest graphics chip in the world, do you want to be the twenty-first horse, or do you want to evaluate the field of twenty and pick the best one? Dell pioneered a new business model that focused on speed of execution and minimum inventory. To this end, the company bypassed the dealer channel, selling products directly to customers over the phone. This eliminated the reseller's markup, costs and risks of carrying large finished good inventories. The model was characterized by high-velocity, low-cost distribution, direct customer relationships, build-to-order, Just-In-Time manufacturing, and products and services aimed at specific market segments. The model had several key advantages. By eliminating the intermediaries, Dell could dramatically reduce its channel costs.

Since every Dell system was built to order, customers got exactly what they asked for. Dell used the knowledge it gleaned from this direct contact to tailor its service and support as well as future offerings. Since materials flowed faster in Dell factories, the latest technology was introduced faster than through the slow-moving indirect channels. As Dell remarks, "If I've got 11 days of inventory and my competitor has 80, and Intel comes out with a new 450-megahertz chip, that means I'm going to get to market 69 days sooner."

Discussion: What is Dell Computer's early success with the direct-sale model?

Chapter 4

Distribution
配送

AESCO's Business Model
AESCO 的商业模式

Since 1979, AESCO had registered strong and steady growth averaging 14.5% per year, soon emerging as a leading distributor of electronics components to **OEMs** and **MROs**.

AESCO provided value in four ways. First, the primary business dealt with "time-place-distribution" of electronic components, i.e. getting the right components to the right person at the right time and place. Second, the company provided assembly and **kitting** services to its customers. Third, AESCO extended attractive payment terms to customers who would have otherwise been lost due to poor credit standings. Finally, AESCO had a pool of employees who made sales calls on behalf of the manufacturers that franchised AESCO.

AESCO primarily performed the traditional distribution function normally associated with distributors. OEMs frequently wanted electronics components in small order quantities that were below the manufacturer's minimum order quantity. They turned to distributors like AESCO, who were willing to "break bulk" by buying large quantities from the manufacturers and

OEM
原始设备制造商
(Original Equipment Manufacturer)

MRO
维护、维修、运行
(Maintenance, Repair&Operation)

kitting
['kɪtɪŋ]
n. 配套采购；配套出售件

自从 1979 年以来，AESCO 取得了每年 14.5% 的稳定而强势的增长，并很快成了为 OEM 和 MRO 提供电子零件的主导供应商。

AESCO 提供四种有价值的服务方式。首先，关于电子零件的"时空配送"，也就是在正确的时间将正确的零件送到正确的地点的正确的人；其次，公司为客户提供加工和配套工具等服务；再次，对于那些由于信用等级低而有可能流失的客户提供了有吸引力的支付条款；最后，公司有大量的员工来代表给予 AESCO 授权的制造商们拓展业务。

AESCO 主要进行与分销商有关的传统的配送业务。OEM 公司经常需要少量的电子零件，但其数量又低于制造商的最小起订量，因此该公司就转向像 AESCO 这样的配送商。AESCO 愿意从制造商那里批量购买，然后拆成较小的订购数量发

shipping smaller order quantities. In recent years, many of AESCO's customers had started demanding JIT delivery, **stipulating** narrow time frames during which AESCO was expected to deliver their orders. OEMs also turned to a single distributor for major portions of their sourcing needs. Thus, an OEM might buy wires and capacitors that originated at different manufacturers but were carried by AESCO. Such **"one-stop"** reduced order processing time and cost at the OEMs and allowed for a smaller purchasing department.

OEMs also turned to AESCO when they needed emergency shipments; AESCO could deliver such emergency requests quickly due to its proximity to customers and since it also carried "safety stock", i.e. an inventory of various components at its warehouse that anticipated such requests.

AESCO specialized in **delivering** small orders. In contrast to large distributors, who were able to offer lower prices for some products (partially due to volume discounts from manufacturers), AESCO offered flexibility in delivery and was willing to accommodate smaller order quantities. The second major element of AESCO's business was value-added subassembly. **In addition to** these streams of business, AESCO augmented the traditional manufacturer's **sales force** by making sales calls on behalf of those manufacturers that had **franchised** them. A recent addition was an in-house

stipulate ['stɪpjuleɪt]
vt. 规定，约定
vi. 明确要求

one-stop [,wʌn'stɒp]
adj. 一站式的

deliver [dɪ'lɪvə]
vt. 发送

in addition to
除……之外

sales force
销售力量，
推销人员

franchise ['fræntʃaɪz]
v. 特许(经营)

送给OEM。最近几年，许多AESCO的客户开始要求及时配送，这使得AESCO在很短的时间内就要发货。OEM也倾向于选择单一的配送商来配送需求的主要部分，这样，一个OEM可能购买来自不同制造商的电线和电容器，但都是由AESCO配送。这样的"一站式"服务减少了OEM的订购时间和成本，使该公司的采购部门规模更小。

当OEM需要急件时，他们也联系AESCO，AESCO之所以能处理这种急件，原因在于其对客户很熟悉并且有安全的库存，也就是基于需求预测的不同零件的库存。

AESCO的专长是发送小批量订单，与一些能提供较低价格产品的大配送商相比(价格低部分是因为制造商的批量折扣)，AESCO的配送更灵活，因为它愿意提供小批量的配送。AESCO业务的第二个主要方面是增值装配。除了这些主要业务之外，AESCO还安排人员代表已授权给他们公司的制造商开展电话营销，增强了该制造商的销售力量。AESCO最近还增设了家庭

telesales department, established to expand sales coverage to areas not served previously.

电话直销部门，这个部门的建立是为了将销售范围扩大到以前没有涉及的区域。

专栏 4-1　OEM

OEM(Original Equipment Manufacturer)是受托厂商按原厂的需求与授权，依特定的条件进行生产。所有产品都完全依照上游厂商的设计来进行制造加工。OEM生产，即代工生产，也称为定点生产，俗称代工，基本含义为品牌生产者不直接生产产品，而是利用自己掌握的关键的核心技术负责设计和开发新产品，控制销售渠道，具体的加工任务通过合同订购的方式委托同类产品的其他厂家生产，之后将所订产品低价买断，并直接贴上自己的品牌商标。这种委托他人生产的合作方式简称OEM，承接加工任务的制造商被称为OEM厂商，其生产的产品被称为OEM产品。可见，定点生产属于加工贸易中的"代工生产"方式，在国际贸易中是以商品为载体的劳务出口。

Learning Objectives【学习目标】

- To understand the definition of distribution.
- To understand the definition of distribution center.
- To learn the distribution process.

Key Terms 【关键词】

distribution	配送	distribution center	配送中心
bulk goods	散装货物	customer-oriented	面向客户
value-added activities	增值活动	distribution process	配送流程

Part 1　Definition of Distribution　配送的定义

Distribution is a logistics end delivery service in which goods move from suppliers to users within a relatively fixed distance and **time span**. It includes both the physical movement of goods and handling of

time span
时间跨度

配送是商品在相对固定的空间和时间段内从供应商向用户移动的物流末端递送服务，包括商品实体的移动和相关手续的办理。

related procedures. Distribution focuses on customer satisfaction and aims at cost reduction. Its operation is often centralized and **integrated** within a specific cover area.

Distribution differs from transport in that:

integrate
['ɪntɪgreɪt]
v. 整合；使……成整体

配送以满足客户为中心并以降低成本为目的，其作业通常是在一个特定的覆盖范围内以集中和一体化的方式完成的。

配送在下列方面有别于运输：

Distribution 配送	Transport 运输
Distribution is usually a end delivery between two places or among more places over a shorter distance, e.g. within a town or several towns within the reach of the operator. 配送通常指两地或两地以上的短途末端运输，如在经营者业务覆盖范围内的一个或数个城镇之内。	Transport is trunk movement between two points/places, usually over a longer distance. 运输指两点或两地之间的干线运输，通常距离较长。
Distribution is customer-oriented. 配送面向客户。	Transport is often place-oriented. 运输通常面向地点。
Distribution is a kind of repeated or reoccurring service. 配送是一种重复性的或多次发生的服务。	Transport is usually a one-time service. 运输通常是一次性的服务。
Distribution often involves complex procedures. 配送经常涉及复杂的手续。	Transport is relatively simple in procedures. 运输手续相对比较简单。

Part 2　Distribution Center　配送中心

Distribution center is a logistics link to fulfill physical distribution as its main function. Generally speaking, it's a large and highly automated center **destined** to receive goods from various plants and suppliers, take orders, fill them efficiently, and deliver goods to customers as quickly as possible.

destine
['destɪn]
v. 预定

配送中心的主要功能就是作为一个物流节点履行物资配送。一般而言，它是一个大型的高度自动化中心，用来接收来自各种工厂和供应商的商品，接受订单，有效地执行订单，并且尽可能快地将货物运送到客户手中。

Unlike a warehouse, however, its **emphasis** is on the moving of goods rather than long-term storage. Practically, it's a short-term storage center located close to a major market to facilitate the rapid processing of orders and shipment of goods to customers.

The differences between distribution centers and warehouses are as follows:

emphasis
['emfəsɪs]
n. 重点

但是,配送中心又不同于仓库,它强调的是商品的流通,而不是进行长期储存。从实践的角度来看,它是一个短期的储存中心,紧临其主要市场,这样便于快速处理订单,并将货物及时运送给客户。

配送中心与仓库的差异如下:

Distribution centers (DCs) 配送中心	Warehouses (Ws) 仓库
DCs handle most products in four cycles, e.g. receiving, storing, shipping, and picking. 配送中心大多有四个循环处理步骤:收货、储存、装运和提取。	Ws handle most products in two cycles, e.g. receiving and shipping. 仓库只有两个循环处理步骤:收货和装运。
DCs perform a great deal of value-added activities, e.g. final assembly. 配送中心进行大量的增值活动,如成品装配。	Ws perform a minimum of value-added activities. 仓库进行的增值活动很少。
DCs collect data in real time. 配送中心实时收集数据。	Ws collect data in batches (generally) (receive and ship goods in batches). 仓库一般分批收集数据(分批收货、装运)。
DCs hold predominantly high-demand items. 配送中心主要储存需求量大的货物。	Ws store all products (slow or fast moving). 仓库储存所有或慢或快的流通货物。
DCs focus on maximizing the profit impact of fulfilling customer (external customer) delivery requirement. 配送中心完成客户(外部客户)送货要求,最大限度地促进利润的最大化。	Ws focus on minimizing the operating costs to meet shipping requirements. 仓库在满足运输需求的前提下强调运营成本最小化。

Part 3   Distribution Process   配送流程

Distribution of goods is one of the core logistics operations. In practice, the logistics distribution mode varies with operators, nature of products, locations, and other factors. Even the same distribution center may adopt a number of differentiated distribution modes in **specific** situations.

In general, a typical distribution center may execute the following operation processes.

- Stock-up

Stock-up of goods is the preparative work **prior to** distribution, and may include sourcing, ordering, purchasing, gathering, replenishing of goods and the related procedures, such as quality inspection, settlements of accounts, **handover**, etc.

- Storage

Storage in the distribution process has two forms: **reserves** and put-away.

Reserves in distribution constitute a **guarantee** for the distributed resources according to the operation requirements in a certain period. Such reserves, great in a quantity, have established structures. Plans can be made to determine the structures and quantity of **rotation** reserves and security reserves, depending on the source and availability of goods.

The other form of storage is put-away,

specific
[spɪˈsɪfɪk]
adj. 特殊的，特定的

prior to
在之前；居先

handover
[ˈhændəʊvə]
n. 移交

reserve [rɪˈzɜːv]
n. 储备，储存

guarantee
[ˌɡærənˈtiː]
n. 保证；担保；保证人；保证书；抵押品

rotation
[rəʊˈteɪʃən]
n. 周转

商品配送是物流的核心作业之一。物流配送模式会因经营者、产品性质、地域等因素的不同而不同，甚至同一配送中心也可能根据具体情况而同时采用若干个差异化的配送模式。

一般来说，典型的配送中心会执行如下作业流程。

- 备货

备货是配送的准备工作，可以包括筹集货源、订货、购货、集货、进货以及质量检验、结算、交接等手续。

- 储存

配送过程中的储存有储备及暂存两种形态。

配送储备是按一定时期内的经营要求，形成对配送资源的保证。这种类型的储备数量大，储备结构也较完善，视货源及到货情况，可以有计划地确定周转储备和安全储备的结构及数量。

另一种储存形态是暂存，

which, after the picking/**groupage** operation, forms **temporary** storage for the dispatch loads, aiming at regulating the rhythms of groupage and delivery. Put-away does not last long.

● Processing

Processing in distribution generally refers to the reprocessing, as per sales requirements, of finished or **semi-finished** products ready for distribution, including:

(1) Segmentation, e.g. cutting big-sized products as per different purposes.

(2) Separate packaging, e.g. repackaging of **bulk goods** or goods in big bales as per the sales requirements.

(3) Selection, e.g. selecting and respective packaging of agricultural by-products as per quality, **specifications**.

(4) **Promotional** packaging, e.g. pairing of free promotional presents.

(5) Labeling, e.g. sticking of price tags, printing of barcodes.

The processing operation completed, the goods are ready for distribution.

● Picking and groupage

Picking and groupage is a unique functional element of distribution which is distinct from other logistics forms. It is also one of the **supportive** tasks vital to the success or failure of distribution. Where there is picking and groupage, there will be marked improvement of the delivery service levels. Picking and groupage is the key element to determine the level of the entire distribution system.

groupage
['gruːpɪdʒ]
n. 货物合并装运

temporary
['tempərəri]
adj. 暂时的，临时的

semi-finished
['semɪfɪnɪʃt]
adj. 半加工的；半制成的

bulk goods
[贸易]
散装货物

specification
[ˌspesɪfɪ'keɪʃən]
n. 规格

promotional
[prəʊ'məʊʃənəl]
adj. 促销的；奖励的

supportive
[sə'pɔːtɪv]
adj. 支持的；支援的；赞助的

即在分拣和配货之后，形成对集散货物的临时存放，其主要目的是调节配货与送货的节奏，暂存时间不会持续很长。

● 配送加工

配送加工一般是指对即将配送的产成品或半成品按销售要求进行再加工，包括：

(1) 分割加工，如对大尺寸产品按不同用途进行切割。

(2) 分装加工，如将散装或大包装的产品按零售要求进行重新包装。

(3) 分选加工，如对农副产品按质量、规格进行分选，并分别包装。

(4) 促销包装，如促销赠品搭配。

(5) 贴标加工，如粘贴价格标签，打印条形码。

加工作业完成后，产品即进入可配送状态。

● 分拣及配货

分拣及配货是配送区别于其他物流形式特有的标志，也是决定配送成败的一项重要的支持性工作。有了分拣及配货就会显著提高送货服务水平，所以分拣及配货是决定整个配送系统水平的关键要素。

- Multi-part loads

Occasionally, the distribution volume of a single customer cannot reach the full payload of the delivery vehicle, which means there is need for the operator to make groupage load for goods from various customers, so that transport capacity can be made full use of. This is called multi-part loads.

Unlike ordinary delivery, the operator can, through multi-part loads, significantly improve the level of delivery and reduce the costs thereof. Multi-part load, as a functional element with **characteristic** of modern distribution, marks a point where modern distribution is significantly different from traditional delivery.

- Shipment in distribution

Shipment in distribution is a form of tail end transport usually over a shorter distance in a smaller scale with road vehicles as its **carriage** tool.

- Delivery service

Shipment of goods to the user does not mean the completion of distribution, because inconsistency occurs from time to time between delivered goods and the user's receipt of goods. This may reduce the previous effort to a total failure.

In order to fulfill secure handover of the delivered goods, the distribution staff should handle handover and receipt **formalities** of the goods, complete settlement of accounts if necessary, listen to customer's

characteristic
[ˌkærəktəˈrɪstɪk]
n. 特征；特性；特色

carriage
[ˈkærɪdʒ]
n. 运输

formality
[fɔːˈmælɪtɪ]
n. 正式手续

- 配装

在单个客户配送数量不能达到车辆的有效运载负荷时，就存在如何集中不同客户的配送货物，进行搭配装载以充分利用运能和运力的问题，这就需要配装。

和一般送货不同，通过配装送货可以大大提高送货水平并降低送货成本，所以配装也是配送系统中有现代特点的功能要素，是现代配送不同于传统送货的重要区别之一。

- 配送运输

配送运输是一种末端运输形式，通常距离较短、规模较小，并用汽车作为其运输工具。

- 送达服务

将配好的货物运输到客户手中还不算配送工作的结束，这是因为偶尔会出现运送的货物和客户签收的货物不一致的情况，使配送前功尽弃。

因此，要圆满地实现运送货物的安全移交，配送人员应当处理相关货物的交接手续，完成必要的结算，听取客户对服务的反馈意见，

| feedback on service and report to the distribution manager that distribution task is completed. | 并向管理人员汇报完成的配送工作。 |

Summary 本章小结

This chapter provides an overview of distribution and distribution center. The differences between distribution center and warehouses are also shown in details. It also introduces distribution process.

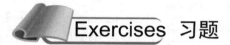

Questions for Review 复习题

1. What is distribution management?
2. Why is distribution management important for a company?
3. Please describe the function of distribution management.

True or False 判断对错

1. Distribution is usually over a shorter distance.
2. DCs handle most products in cycles, e.g. receiving, storing, and picking.
3. Picking and groupage is the key element to determine the level of the entire distribution system.
4. Process in distribution refers to the reprocessing finished products ready for distribution.
5. Distribution can, through multi-part loads, significantly improve the level of delivery and reduce the costs thereof.

Topic for Discussion 讨论话题

Joe Bailey called you at Eurosped on his mobile phone. He is now at the place shown on this simplified map of Leipzig. Use expressions from the below to direct him to the Neue Messe.

Take the motorway | northbound.
 | southbound.
 | heading for ...
 | in the direction of ...

Leave the motorway at | junction number ...
 | the exit signposted ...

Turn | right | at the | traffic lights.
 | left | | crossing.
Go straight on | | | junction.

Take the | first | turning on the | left.
 | second | | right.

Follow the signs for ...

It's in (the) ... street.

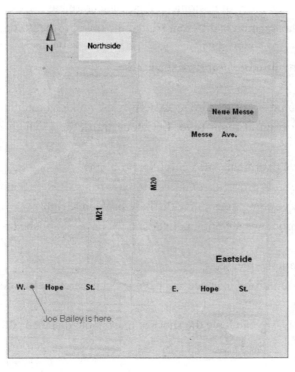

Logistics English Dialogue 物流英语对话

How Do We Operate the Distribution Network?

A: I understand distribution is a core component of logistics operation.

B: True! Without distribution, the logistics link would not be complete.

A: And the product would not reach the end users.

B: Exactly.

A: But what activities does the distribution process involve?

B: In general, it involves stock-up, storage, processing, picking/groupage, shipment and delivery service.

A: What do you mean by stock-up?

B: It means getting goods available for the next process.

A: How about groupage?

B: If the items from a single customer cannot reach the full payload of the delivery vehicle, we may group items from several customers.

A: In order to make full use of the vehicle capacity.

B: That's right.

A: We have a great quantity of customers. And each store has its specific requirements. They order different items; the location is different so that the travel route is complex; and delivery time also varies.

B: In fact, there are far more problems than these.

A: For example...

B: Occasionally some stores require us to deliver the goods at midnight. This means we must have someone on duty even at night time. Let alone traffic jam, which may delay the delivery service.

A: Then how do we coordinate such complex problems?

B: Well, we tackle such problems on a case-to-case basis. It is difficult to generalize.

A: But we must have some rules to tackle these problems, right?

B: Most of these problems are anticipative, and we have established measures and techniques to cope with them.

A: Give me an example, please.

B: Take vehicle routing for instance we have special personnel to design the route for each delivery task.

A: I see. In this way, we can have the shortest reasonable distance and minimal travel time.

B: Exactly.

Chapter 4 Distribution
配送

Case Study 案例分析题

Catering Services Distribution

ABC Catering Services Ltd. was founded in 1982 to provide catering services to major international airlines in the Asia Pacific Rim(环太平洋地区). It has long recognized needs to compete effectively in its key markets in the Pacific Rim.

The business delivers 44 million meals each year to airlines. It has totally four kitchens located in HK, Shenzhen PRC, Ang Mo Kio Singapore and Seoul South Korea respectively. ABC uses 250 tons of chicken, 73 tons of eggs, and 38000 cases of wines and champagnes a year. Currently, it has over 10000 employees within the group.

Its replenishment activities mainly involve the Procurement Office at TST, Distribution Center (DC) at the HK International Airport, and the four kitchens fax orders to the replenishment office biweekly. Orders are checked against the inventory in the distribution center, processed and faxed to suppliers. The suppliers will supply raw materials to the DC where materials are forwarded to four kitchens by means of mainly air, and then road and lastly sea. Kitchens at the four locations manufacture catering meals, pack and deliver to airlines at local airports. Most of surplus items will be retuned to the DC for repackaging, and the rest will be stored in the local kitchens.

Currently there is no sophisticated database or system used other than Excel spread sheets. Due to many orders and heavy workload, it takes about one week to process orders at the Procurement Office at TST. Each Kitchen has to keep track of business data such as inventory, lead times, transportation costs, and so on. This information will be reported to the Procurement Office every two weeks on the same day of placing orders by e-mails.

The delivery lead time from suppliers to Distribution Center is usually half day. However, the lead time from the Distribution Center to each kitchen is various from 1 day to 2 weeks. There is not much concern about the distribution to HK and Shenzhen kitchens. However, the long lead time in the delivery to AMK and Seoul kitchens ranging from 1 to 2 weeks would either cause trouble in delivery to airline customers on time or trigger many urgent orders, which have higher associated costs. Why? The reason is that the company has an arrangement with XYZ Cargo to carry materials to Seoul and AMK at big discount rate so long as they can't sell the space and weight elsewhere. In other words, when XYZ Cargo's performance is good, and payloads are full, materials are left behind sometimes for days until the delay can no longer be accepted, and space or alternatives carriers are sought. This will affect the downstream performance and delivery on time to airline customers.

The primary task for the kitchens is to make sure of the availability of quality and hygiene food. Because of the delay in delivery of materials, the Catering Manager in each kitchen very often replace urgent orders he feels needed and informs the replenishment office later. This often leads to overstocking and higher rush order cost.

Toby D. Leung, the new CEO, hired LCP, specialized supply chain and logistics consulting firm, to help him undertake diagnosis and make recommendations to change.

LCP has suggested several recommendations to ABC Catering and help them undertake the implementation. Over a period of three months, inventory cost from the Distribution Center dropped by 3 million below normal trends to 2.5 million and inventory at each kitchen was kept below 0.5 million. This inventory saving was transferred directly to the profit and loss account.

The order processing time at the Procurement Office was reduced to 1 day from 1 week and the replenishment cycle shortens from 2 weeks to 1 week. The lead time from Distribution Center to Ang Mo Kio kitchen and Bangkok kitchen is down to 2 days from the original 1 or 2 weeks. Thus, service performance to airline customers from kitchens improved and urgent orders were significantly down to zero, because of the improvement in supply chain reliability.

Discussions:

1. What are the problems faced by ABC Catering?
2. What are the causes to these problems?
3. If you were the consultant from LCP, what recommendations would you give to ABC?
4. What are the possible achievements that you can think of in this case?

Chapter 5

Packaging

包装

Pay Attention to Packaging Charges
关注包装费用

If you're getting hit with oversize or special-handling **charge**s, investigate whether changing your packaging could help you avoid those extra costs, suggested by Doug Kahl, director of sales and business development for AFMSA, a Portland, Ore., **consultancy** that specializes in parcel shipping. "Compare the size and dimension of the item being shipped to the box it's being shipped in," he says, "if you're using a large box with a lot of protective **dunnage**, decide whether the additional oversize costs are worthwhile compared to the risk of damage posed by reduced packaging." In some cases, he adds, the item itself may qualify for "Oversize 1" but the packaging converts it to a more expensive "Oversize 2 or 3."

For irregularly shaped parcels, it may be possible to switch to packaging that would change them to "**conveyable**" format and eliminate the extra handling charge. At $6 a package, those savings can be considerable.

What if the oversize charges are a significant burden but it's impossible to change your packaging? For air express

charge [tʃɑ:dʒ]
n. 费用

consultancy [kən'sʌltənsɪ]
n. 咨询公司

dunnage ['dʌnɪdʒ]
n. 衬垫；填充物

conveyable [kən'veɪəbəl]
adj. 可传达的；可搬运的；可转让的

位于美国俄勒冈州波特兰市专门从事包裹运输咨询服务的AFMSA咨询公司的销售和商务拓展部主管 Doug Kahl 建议，如果你正遇到要被征收超大附加费或特殊搬运费的问题，你可以研究一下是否可以通过改变包装来避免这些附加费用。"比较要装入盒中的货物与盒子本身的大小和尺寸，"他说，"如果你使用一只大盒子和大量防护性的填充物要花额外的超大费用，但减少包装又会面临损坏的风险时，那就要衡量一下额外的超大费用是否值得。"在一些情形下，他接着说，货物本身就达到"超大1型"的级别，加上包装就转变为更贵的"超大2或3型"。

对于那些形状不规则的包裹，你可以将包装转换成适合传输的包装类型，这样就可以避免支付每件6美元的附加费，节省的费用会

shipments, try negotiating a higher **dimensional** factor, Tim Sailor, a principal of transportation specialists Navigo Consulting says. The dimensional factor is a **parcel**'s weight-to-size ratio, or its **density**. The lower the density, the more expensive it is for the carrier to handle and the more you'll pay; carriers bill low-density packages on their "chargeable weight," as if they were heavier.

One of Sailor's clients, for example, was shipping medical **specimens** in packaging filled with **dry ice**. "They were getting killed with dimensional charges, but they needed that much packaging to accommodate the dry ice," he says. After negotiating the dimensional factor from 184 to 250, the chargeable weight was reduced from 12 pounds to 9 pounds, for average annual savings of $150,000, he says.

dimensional
[dɪˈmenʃənəl, daɪ-]
adj. 尺寸的

parcel [ˈpɑːsl]
n. 包裹，小包

density [ˈdensətɪ]
n. 密度

specimen [ˈspesəmən]
n. 样品，样本；标本

dry ice
干冰，固态二氧化碳

相当可观。

如果超大附加费数额巨大而又无法改变货物的包装时，该怎么办？专门从事运输咨询业的 Navigo Consulting 公司的负责人 Tim Sailor 认为：对于航空快运的承运人而言应尽量争取降低包裹的比重系数。比重系数是包裹的重量与大小的比率，也就是它的密度。密度越低，承运人收取的搬运费越高，客户付的钱就越多。承运人按照"可征收重量"而非实际重量对低密度包裹计费，好像它们真的更重了。

例如，Sailor 的一个客户要寄医学样品，样品必须放在充满干冰的包装中。他说："比重收费制要了他们的命，而他们需要那么大的包装来容纳干冰。"客户通过与航空公司谈判，将包裹比重从 184 谈到 250 后，征收重量从 12 磅降到 9 磅，每年节省了 150000 美元。

Learning Objectives 【学习目标】

- To understand different kinds of packaging.
- To learn the main functions of packaging.
- To know about the importance of packing mark.
- To get familiar with package materials.

Key Terms 【关键词】

packaging	包装	protection	保护
sales packaging	销售包装	transport packaging	运输包装
shipping mark	运输标识	identification mark	识别标识
handling instruction	储运标识		

Part 1　Introduction of Packaging 包装概述

1. Definition of packaging

In recent years, the significance of packing has been increasingly recognized, and today the widespread use of packing is truly a major competitive force in the struggle for markets.

● Packaging methods

Packaging is the technique of preparing goods for distribution. Packaging refers to creation of a pack or a packaging unit (i.e. **receptacle** and any other components or materials necessary to perform its containment function) by combination of product with the package, applying methods of packaging with packaging machines or devices by hand.

● Packing elements

The selection or construction of the shipping container and the **assembling** of items or packages therein, including any necessary blocking, bracing, or **cushioning**, weatherproofing, exterior strapping, and marking of shipping container for identification of contents.

receptacle
[rɪ'septəkl]
n. 容器

assemble
[ə'sembl]
v. 集合，聚集；装配；收集

cushion
['kuʃən]
n. 垫子；起缓冲作用之物

1. 包装的定义

近年来，包装的重要性逐渐被认可，当前，广泛使用的包装已成为产品在市场竞争中的主要手段。

● 包装方法

包装是产品在进入流通过程前所采用的技术措施。按照一定的技术方法，采用包装机械或手工操作将产品和包装物制成包裹或一个包装单位(例如，用容器或其他必需的材料体现其包装功能)。

● 包装的要素

包装包括装运容器的选择或结构设计，并将产品(货物)集装或置放在包装中，包括产品与产品之间必要的隔离、支撑、缓冲、防晒防潮措施，还有外部捆扎以及包装标识。

2. Types of Packages

- Sales packaging

Sales packaging is normally with **decoration** and explanation. They are direct printing or sticking on the label or barcode. Some products need to print the trade mark, brand name, place of original as well as specification and instruction.

- Transport packaging

Transport packaging is also called outer packing. It can be divided into separated piece packing and integrated packing. Separated packing means the unit to pack the goods such as cases, drums, bags, **tins** and **rolls**. Integrated packing such as containers and **pallets** which can ship the goods together.

3. Functions of Packaging

Packaging fulfills different functions.

- To protect and preserve a product from physical, chemical and **mechanical** damage;
- To facilitate ease of handling and transport;
- To communicate information, e.g. safety instructions;
- To act as a marketing aid, through appearance and presentation;
- In addition to product protection, packages should be easy to handle, convenient to store, readily identifiable, secure and of a shape that makes best use of space.

decoration [ˌdekəˈreɪʃən]
n. 装饰，装潢；装饰品

tin [tɪn]
n. 罐头，罐；马口铁

roll [rəʊl]
n. 卷，卷形物；名单

pallet [ˈpælət]
n. 托盘，货板

mechanical [mɪˈkænɪkəl]
adj. 机械的；力学的

2. 包装的分类

- 销售包装

销售包装应有适宜的装饰图案和必要的文字说明。它们通常直接印刷在包装上，或采用在货物上粘贴标签、条形码等方式。某些商品的销售包装上还印有商标、品牌、产地、用途说明和使用方法等内容。

- 运输包装

运输包装又称外包装，分为单件运输包装和集合运输包装。前者是指在运输过程中作为一个计件单位的包装，例如箱、桶、袋、罐、捆等；后者是指将若干单件运输包装组合成一件大包装，常见的有集装箱和托盘等。

3. 包装的功能

包装实现不同的功能。

- 保护产品，使其免受物理、化学及机械损伤。
- 方便装卸搬运，方便运输。
- 传达信息，如安全说明。
- 通过外观呈现吸引消费者，从而促进市场的推广。

- 除具备保护产品的功能外，包装还应当易于搬运，方便存储，可随时识别，安全性强并且具有可充分利用空间的形状。

Part 2　Packing Materials　包装材料

Except for the cargo in bulk, such as grain, coal and ore, and the nuded cargo, such as steel bars and wood, most goods need adequate packing for the purpose of transport and sales. In order to avoid damage that occurred during transit in ocean transportation, strong packing is needed to withstand rough handling.

为方便运输和销售，除散装货如谷物、煤炭、矿砂，或裸装货如钢材、木材等商品外，大多数商品都需要适当包装。特别是在海运又需转运的情况下，为了避免货物在搬运、装卸和运输过程中因振动、碰撞、挤压等造成损伤，必须要有牢固的包装(以承受这些操作)。

1. Plastic

Plastics are used because they are:
- Easy to shape and color
- Cheap
- Flexible
- Good **insulators** of heat
- Light
- Strong (high strength-to-density ratios)
- **Hygienic**
- Non-rusting
- Good resistance to acids, **alkalis**, and solvents

insulator
['ɪnsjuleɪtə, 'ɪnsə-]
n. [物] 绝缘体

hygienic
[haɪ'dʒiːnɪk, haɪdʒɪ'enɪk]
adj. 卫生的，保健的

alkali
['ælkəlaɪ]
n. 碱；可溶性无机盐

1. 塑料

塑料包装的原因：
- 易成型和上色
- 价格低
- 弹性好
- 具有良好的绝热性
- 重量轻
- 牢固(比强度高)
- 无毒
- 不易腐蚀
- 具有良好的耐酸碱性和不易溶解性

2. Aluminium

Aluminium is made from bauxite (it takes about 4 kg of bauxite to produce 1 kg of pure aluminium). Pure aluminium is a soft, **silvery white**, relatively light metal, which conducts heat and electricity easily. It is used for cans and **foil**. Thick foils constitute a complete barrier to all gases (thinner ones have **pin-holing**). Aluminium can be recycled. Producing new aluminium cans from used ones saves up 95% of the energy needed to produce cans from raw materials.

3. Glass

Glass is clear, **rigid**, chemically inert, heat resistant, resistant to internal pressure, and a complete barrier to **water vapour** and gases. Glass can be recycled (reasonably clean, and separated as clear, green and brown glass in the bottle bank). Up to one-third of the energy required to make new glass can be saved, but transport costs reduce the total energy saved.

4. Steel

Steel consists of iron (can be tested with a **magnet**). Bare steel **corrodes** readily when in contact with moisture. Therefore, a layer of tin is deposited on the can (thicker on the inside where more protection is needed). Steel can be recycled (cans should be cleaned). Savings in energy can be about 75% compared to

silvery white
银白色

foil [fɔɪl]
n. 箔，金属薄片

pin-hole
n. 销孔，针孔

rigid ['rɪdʒɪd]
adj. 坚硬的

water vapour
水蒸气，水汽

magnet ['mægnɪt]
n. 磁铁；[电磁] 磁体；磁石

corrode [kə'rəʊd]
vi. 受腐蚀；起腐蚀作用

2. 铝

铝是以铝矾土为原料制成的(大约 4 千克铝矾土生产 1 千克的纯铝)。纯铝比较柔软，呈现银白色，是相对较轻的金属，易导电和导热。其可以制成罐头外包装(或盒)和铝箔。厚的铝箔可以阻碍所有的气体(薄的铝箔有针孔)。铝可以再循环。利用旧铝罐生产新的铝罐可以比用原材料生产铝罐节约95%的能源。

3. 玻璃

玻璃是一种透明、坚硬、化学稳定性高、耐热、耐内压力、不透湿和不透气的材料。玻璃可以再循环(相对干净的空瓶在回收箱中按透明、绿色和褐色玻璃分开)。回收玻璃用于生产新玻璃时，可以节约近三分之一的能源，但是高运输成本抵减了节约的能源。

4. 钢

钢由铁组成(可以用磁铁来检测)。当接触湿气时，裸钢很容易被腐蚀，因此在铁罐上镀一层锡(当需要更多保护时，在内部涂上较厚一层锡)。钢可以再循环(罐头要清洗干净)。与生产新钢

producing new steel.

5. Paper

Modern paper is almost always made from **wood pulp**, which can be obtained from many plants, depending on the required strength of the paper (longer **fibers** give stronger paper). Paper may be **bleached** (white), unbleached (brown) or colored. The surface can have different types of finishing or **glazing**. Board is heavy paper made of several layers bonded together. Paper can be recycled. As paper is recycled, the fibers get shorter and weaker (recycling maximally 4 or 5 times).

6. Multilayer Materials

Frequently different materials are used together in layers to meet all the needs of the product inside. A plastic material can be **metallised**, or paper can be protected outwards by a plastic layer and inwards by an aluminium layer.

Some packagings (e.g. **tomato ketchup** plastic bottles) have even more layers: a layer suitable for food contact; a layer to stop gas exchange; an outer protective layer, which can be made from recycled materials; tie layers between the other layers. Other layers may protect the content from light, or help sealing of the packaging.

Multilayer is difficult to recycle due to their makeup, but some recycling companies chip them up and use them for plastic chipboard. Alternatively their **fate** is the **dustbin**.

---

wood pulp
[纸] 木浆; 木纤维; 木质纸浆

fiber ['faɪbə]
n. 纤维; 光纤

bleach [bliːtʃ]
vi. 变白, 漂白

glaze [gleɪz]
vt. 装玻璃于; 上釉于

metallise ['metəlaɪz]
vt. 金属化

tomato ketchup
番茄酱

fate [feɪt]
n. 命运

dustbin ['dʌstbɪn]
n. 垃圾箱

材相比可以节约将近 75% 的能源。

5. 纸

现代的纸几乎都是由木浆制成，木浆可以从许多植物获得，根据纸的强度选择不同的木纤维(纤维长的制出的纸强度更高)。纸可以漂白(白色的)、不漂白(褐色)或染色。表面可以有不同类型的上光。纸板是由多层纸黏结而成的厚纸。纸能被再循环。当纸被再循环时，纤维变得更短而且强度变弱(最多再循环 4~5 次)。

6. 复合材料

通常不同的材料以多层的形式复合在一起来满足产品包装的需求。塑料材料可以镀上金属或者是在纸的外表覆上一层塑料薄膜，里面覆上一层铝薄膜。

一些包装(如番茄酱的塑料瓶)有很多层：一层适合与食品接触；一层阻止气体交流；外保护层可以由回收材料制成；紧固层在其他各层之间。其他层可以保护产品免受光照，或有助于密封包装。

复合包装材料因其成分而难以再循环使用，但一些回收公司把它们压碎制成塑料硬板，而无法回收的复合包装材料只能丢弃。

Part 3　Packing Mark　包装标识

Packing Mark is the mark to facilitate the cargo, transfer, stock or the mark to identify the goods and avoid damage. Packing mark includes shipping mark, **indicative** mark, warning mark and so on.

indicative
[ɪnˈdɪkətɪv]
adj. 象征的；指示的；表示的

abbreviation
[əˌbriːvɪˈeɪʃən]
n. 缩写；缩写词

包装标识是为了方便货物运输、装卸及储存，便于识别货物和防止货物损坏而在货物外包装上刷写的标识。包装标识主要包括运输标识、指示性标识、警告性标识等。

1. Shipping Mark

Shipping marks are made of some numbers, characters or some simple words. Normally they will be printed on the outer packing. The contents of shipping mark are as follows:

- **Abbreviations** or shorted forms of consignee's name
- Reference Marks
- Destination
- Marks of pieces

2. Identification Mark

It is also called subsidiary mark. For example:

CON. NO. : 94CL-H08
ART. NO. : 904A
COLOR : NAVY/GREY
SIZE :
N.W. : 11.3 KG
G.W. : 16.4 KG
MEAS. : 45.5×52×55.5cm
Country of origin: MADE IN CHINA

N.W.
(net weight)
净重

G.W.
(gross weight)
毛重

1. 运输标识

俗称唛头，由一些阿拉伯数字、字母或简单的文字组成，通常印刷在外包装明显的部位。运输标识包括以下部分：

- 收货人的名称缩写或简称
- 参考号码
- 目的地
- 件数

2. 识别标识

识别标识又称附属标识，例如：

合同号：94CL-H08
货号：904A
颜色：藏青色/青色
尺码：
净重：11.3 kg
毛重：16.4 kg
尺码：45.5 cm×52 cm×55.5 cm
生产国别：中国制造

3. Indicative Mark

This kind of mark is used to remind the relative workers of the items for attention when they load, unload, carry and store the goods, such as "handle with care" "keep dry".

4. Warning Mark

It is also called dangerous cargo mark, which is brushed clearly and definitely on the shipping packing of the **inflammable**, explosive, poisonous, corrosive goods, so as to give warnings to the workers.

inflammable
[ɪnˈflæməbl]
adj. 易燃的；易怒的

3. 指示性标识

指示性标识(又称操作标识)，用来指示装卸、运输和保管人员在作业时需要注意的事项，以保证货物的安全，如"小心轻放""保持干燥"等。

4. 警告性标识

警告性标识又称危险品标识，是指在易燃、易爆、有毒、有腐蚀性等危险品的运输外包装上的一些醒目的标识，以警告有关人员不得掉以轻心。

专栏 5-1　标准运输标识

联合国欧洲经济委员会简化国际贸易程序工作组，在国际标准化组织和国际货物装卸协调协会的支持下，制定了一项运输标识标准，向各国推荐使用。该标准运输标识包括以下几种。

(1) 收货人或买方名称的英文缩写字母或简称。

(2) 参考号，如订单号、发票号、信用证号、进口许可证号、合同号等。

(3) 目的地。如果中途需要转船或转运，则应加列"转船"字样和转运地名称。

(4) 件号。在货物付运时，货主按照顺序要对每件货物进行编号，件号标识一般用 1/100 或 2/100 这种形式表示，其中分母表示该批货物的总件数，分子表示该件货物在整批货物中的编号，也可以用 1~100 这种形式表示，目的是便于核查货物数量。

标准运输标识由 4 行组成，每行不超过 17 个字母(包括数字和符号)，不采用几何图形。只能用拉丁字母 A~Z、阿拉伯数字 0~9、句号、连字符、圆括号、斜线和逗号。

唛头示例：

SGL　　　　　　　　——收货人缩写
88/S/C-179345　　　　——参考号码
NEW YORK　　　　　——目的港名称
NO. 1~500　　　　　 ——箱号或件数

专栏 5-2　　包装搬运图示标识

序　号	标识名称	标识图形	含　义
1	易碎物品		运输包装件内装易碎品，因此搬运时应小心轻放
2	禁用手钩		搬运运输包装件时，禁止使用手钩
3	向上		表明运输包装件的正确位置是竖直向上
4	怕晒		表明运输包装件不能直接照晒
5	远离放射源及热源		用于指示需远离放射源及热源的运输包装件
6	怕雨		包装件怕雨淋
7	重心		表明一个单元货物的重心
8	禁止翻滚		不能翻滚运输包装
9	此面禁用手推车		搬运货物时，此面禁放于手推车上
10	禁用叉车		不能用升降叉车搬运的包装件
11	由此夹起		表明装运货物时夹钳放置的位置
12	此处不能卡夹		表明装卸货物时此处不能用夹钳夹持
13	堆码重量极限		表明该运输包装件所能承受的最大重量极限
14	堆码层数极限		相同包装的最大堆码层数，n 表示层数极限
15	禁止堆码		该包装件不能堆码并且其上也不能放置其他负载
16	由此吊起		起吊货物时挂链条的位置
17	温度极限		表明运输包装件应该保持的温度极限

Part 4　Specimen Letters 信函范例

1. Packing Instructions

May 21, 2019
Dear Mr. Han,

Packing Instructions (Order No.12402)

　　We would like to give the packing instructions for the above order of wine glasses.
　　The ordered goods need to be wrapped up by corrugated paper and packed in wooden cases with excelsior. Please limit the weight of each wooden case to 50 kg. All cases need to be tied in stacks of three.
　　The above packing requirements help reduce the risk of damage during delivery. If you have any questions, please contact me directly.

　　Yours sincerely,

　　Tianming Liu (Ms.)
　　Manager

1. 包装指示

韩先生：

　　包装指示(订单编号：12402)

　　本公司欲对以上玻璃酒杯订货提出包装要求。
　　请先以瓦楞纸包装，然后装入木箱内，以细刨花填塞。所有木箱的重量以 50 千克为限，木箱以三个为一组，用铁条捆起。
　　以上包装方式是为了减少玻璃杯在运输途中损坏的机会。如对此有任何疑问，请直接与本人联络。

经理

刘天明
2019 年 5 月 21 日

2. Marking Instructions

May 28, 2019
Dear Mr. Han,

Marking Instructions (Order No.12402)

　　With reference to the above order of wine-glasses, we would like to give you the marking instructions.
　　The mark including our company initials,

2. 标记指示

韩先生：

　　标记指示(订单编号：12402)

　　就以上玻璃酒杯订货，本公司将给出标记指示。
　　请于包装木箱上标明本公司的缩写名称、目的港、订单编号、"B

port of destination, order number, a "B" label and handling instructions should be listed as below:

SW
DOVER, ENGLAND
WB0329
"B"
Glassware, please don't throw

Please follow the above marking instructions and notice us by fax when the shipment arrangement is completed.

Yours sincerely,

Tianming Liu (Ms.)
Manager

字图案及"小心处理"之类的字句，格式如下：

盛威
英国多佛港
WB0329
"B"
玻璃器皿，请勿乱掷

请按以上格式在该批装运的货品上印上标记。装货完成后，请传真通知本公司。

经理

刘天明
2019 年 5 月 28 日

3. Completion of Packing

June 16, 2019
Dear Ms. Liu,

Completion of Packing (Order No.12402)

We are pleased to inform you that the above order of wineglasses has been packed as requested.

The wooden cases were marked with your company initials, port of destination, order number, mark "B" and handling instructions. The packing charge was covered by the freight.

The goods were shipped by Vessel Wilson on June 15.

Yours sincerely,

Qiang Han (Mr.)
Manager

3. 包装完成

刘小姐：

包装完成(订单编号：12402)

贵公司以上订单的玻璃酒杯，本公司已经依照要求包装妥当。

木箱上印有公司缩写名称、目的港、订单编号及"B"字图案作为主要标记，并按指示加上"小心处理"之类的字句。包装费用包括在运费内。

该批货品已于 6 月 15 日由"威尔逊"号轮船运出。

经理

韩强
2019 年 6 月 16 日

Summary 本章小结

This chapter provides an overview of logistics packaging technology, emphasizes the functions of packaging, package materials and the importance of packing mark. It also deals with letters about packing instructions, marking instructions and completion of packing.

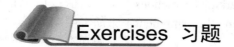
Exercises 习题

Questions for Review 复习题

1. What are the main functions of packaging?
2. Can you name some of the most commonly used packing materials?
3. Why is adequate marking essential?
4. What kind of information should be delivered by packing instructions?

True or False 判断对错

1. Packages should be easy to handle, convenient to store, readily identifiable, secure and of a shape that makes best use of space.
2. As paper is recycled, the fibers get longer and stronger.
3. Packing mark is the only way to facilitate and identify the goods as well as avoiding damage.
4. Indicative mark is used to remind the relative workers of the items for attention when they load, unload, carry and store the goods, such as "handle with care" "keep dry".
5. Warning mark is also called dangerous cargo mark.

Topic for Discussion 讨论话题

Here are some types of packing which are often used.
- A bale is formed when goods are press-packed and wrapped like a parcel in hessian or plastic sheeting and then banded.
- A barrel or cask is for transporting liquids. Traditional barrels are made of wood with horizontal metal bands.
- A carton or cardboard box is the most usual type of packing. It may be filled with

polystyrene, foam or plastic bubble wrapping.
- A chest is a metal box.
- A crate is a wooden box. It may be closed, open or skeleton.
- A drum is a round metal container that stands upright for transporting liquid.
- A pallet is a wooden base onto which goods can be strapped for easy lifting by fork-lift truck.
- A sack is a large bag made of jute, hessian or plastic.

1. Name these types of packing.

    a   b   c

    d   e   f

2. Explain which type of packing would be suitable for these goods.

Note: more than one type of packing may be possible or necessary.

a	sherry	e	computers
b	cotton material	f	machine oil
c	flowers	g	a car engine
d	coffee beans	h	strawberries

Logistics English Dialogue 物流英语对话

Talking About the Subject of Packaging

(A, a businessman from Germany, is talking about the subject of packaging with B, the marketing manager of a company in China.)

A: How are they packed? Please tell me in details.

B: Well, they are packed in boxes of one dozen each, 100 boxes to the carton. The dimensions of the carton are 17 cm high, 30 cm wide and 50 cm long. The volume then is about 0.026 cubic meters.

A: How about the weight?

B: The gross weight is 23.5 kg, and the net is 22.5 kg. You see, the tare weight is one kilogram only.

A: So the ocean freight is charged by weight, not by measurement.

B: Exactly.

A: By the way, what kind of strap do you use for the cartons?

B: Plastic ones.

A: That's good. Plastic straps are light and strong.

B: We always see to it that our customers are guaranteed economical as well as seaworthy packages.

A: OK. We'll see if there's any chance of business.

B: All right. I hope to hear from you soon.

Case Study 案例分析题

Bubble Wrap

Bubble wrap is a kind of flexible plastic sheeting containing numerous small air pockets, used in cushioning items during shipment. Standard average bubble diameter is 6.0～25.4 mm and height about 4 mm.

Bubble wrap is lightweighted, water resistant, reusable, non-scratching, and, commonly used for packing fragile items. So, it is also called "bubble pack".

How is bubble wrap packaging made?

(1) Bubble wrap starts with polyethylene (plastic) resin, in the form of beads about the size of pea gravel.

(2) The beads go into an extruder—a long cylinder with a screw inside that runs its entire length.

(3) As the screw is turned, heat builds up and the resin melts into liquid that is squeezed out of the cylinder into two stacked sheets of clear plastic films.

(4) One layer of the film is wrapped around a drum with holes punched in it, and suction is applied drawing one web of film into the holes that form the bubbles.

(5) The second layer of film is then laminated over the first so that when the two films are joined, they stick together and trap the air in the bubbles.

(6) This may sound easy. But polyethylene is a porous material like a sponge. Air can easily leak out through the pores, which tends to limit the cushioning ability of the packaging. Realizing this, some manufacturing companies such as Sealed Air started using a Saran coating to seal the air in the bubbles. Eventually, a method of encapsulating an air retention barrier in the polyethylene during the extrusion process was developed. This process is a trade secret of Sealed Air Corporation.

Tips for proper use of Bubble Wrap

When you are using Bubble Wrap as a cushioning material, make sure of using enough wrap so that all sides and corners are protected.

Make sure that there is at least two inches of bubble padding between your product and each wall of the box.

You also want to make sure of using enough wrap (or other void fill material in conjunction with Bubble Wrap) to eliminate movement of the packaged item when you shake the box. When you are done with packaging your product, shake it. If you feel the product moving, you need to add more packaging materials.

Unusual use

- Bubble Wrap burglar alarm

Make a burglar alarm for your home. Lay Bubble Wrap on the floor inside your doors and windows. When a thief breaks in and walks across the floor, the "pop-pop-pop-pop-pop-pop-pop" will alert you to the intruder.

- Bubble head

Improvise a football or motorcycle helmet. Wrap massive quantities of Bubble Wrap around your head and seal in place with clear packaging tape (or duct tape). If Bubble Wrap can protect a hand-painted egg shipped from Czechoslovakia across the Atlantic, it can protect your head when it hits asphalt.

CAUTION: The specific amount of Bubble Wrap required for providing adequate protection has not yet been determined.

- Insect Repellent

Bubble Wrap Insect Repellent prevents mosquito bites on arms and legs by covering your extremities in Bubble Wrap. When mosquitoes do try to bite you, the Bubble Wrap bubble will pop and the tiny explosion of air will send the mosquito spiraling through the air.

- Sweet Dreams

Sleeping while camping can be a real pain in the back, unless you are carrying a light six-foot roll of Bubble Wrap as a mat to place under your sleeping bag. Or fold a twelve-foot long piece of Bubble Wrap in half and use duct tape the sides to make the padded-sleeping bag of your dreams.

CAUTION: If you are sleeping on the beach, high tide may cause you to float out to sea.

- Bubble Wrap Instead of Cash

Impress your date by padding your wallet with a piece of Bubble Wrap behind your money. It will look like you have a lot more money than you actually do. Or just impress your date with the fact that you always carry around a trusty piece of Bubble Wrap.

Discussion:

1. How many advantages does Bubble Wrap have?
2. Could you give a new example to illustrate how to make use of Bubble Wrap?

Chapter 6

Warehousing
仓储

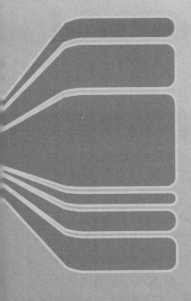

Web Firms Go on Warehouse Building Boom
网络公司使仓库发展突飞猛进

The Internet's top retailers aren't **sneering at** giant warehouse anymore. In contrast they are building them. This wasn't supposed to happen. Much of the early excitement about electronic commerce involved the belief that companies could serve millions of customers without needing anything approaching the infrastructure of the Sears or Wal-Mart. E-commerce companies were supposed to be incredibly efficient **clusters** of computer programmers, who used outside subcontractors to handle such **dreary** tasks as keeping inventory, filling orders and handling customer-service issues. But now online merchants are discovering that if they don't control their own warehouse and shipping, their reliability **ratings** with customers can turn dismal. Amazon.com, for example, is in the midst of a $300 million distribution center initiative that involves building giant facilities in Nevada, Kentucky and Kansas to handle its inventory of books, music, toys and electronics. An online grocery retailer, Webvan Group Inc. has placed a $1 billion order with Bechtel Group for

sneer at
嘲笑；蔑视

cluster ['klʌstə]
n. 群

dreary ['drɪərɪ]
adj. 沉闷的，枯燥的

rating ['reɪtɪŋ]
n. 等级；等级评定

著名的网络零售商已不再嘲笑庞大的仓储空间。相反，它们也在建造大型仓库。这种事情以往是想不到的。对于电子商务，人们早先表现得有点过分兴奋，以为电子商务公司无须建造像西尔斯或者沃尔玛那样的地面基础设施，就可为数百位顾客提供服务；大家原来认为电子商务公司只需聚集一大批工作效率惊人的计算机程序员就行了，因为这些程序员可以委托外部承包商，让他们来处理商品库存、采购及售后服务之类的苦差事。但是，现在网络商家开始认识到，如果不能控制自己的商品库存以及运送业务，顾客对其信任度就会下降。例如，亚马逊公司目前就正在考虑投资 3 亿美元，在内华达、肯塔基和堪萨斯州建造大型配送中心及相关设施，以便管理自己的图书、音像制品、玩

giant warehouse in 26 cities across the US. And other electronic merchants such as eToys Inc. and Barnesandnolbe.com are pushing ahead with big warehouse projects as well.

Such investments may be essential if e-commerce companies hope to build up a base of **loyal** customers, says Steve Johnson, co-director of the e-commerce program at Anderson Consulting. "Customer acquisition costs are quite high for these companies, and the only way to get a pay-off is to get a lot of repeated business from people," he says. "One bad experience and you have **blown it** forever." But Internet companies face a steep learning **curve** as they try to master the shipping and warehouse business. Books and compact disks can be **shunted** through a warehouse without much trouble, but bulky, odd-size items such as toys and electronics are a lot more difficult. Also, customers' **return rate** can be as high as 30 percent in categories such as apparel, posing big challenges in handling such merchandise.

loyal [ˈlɔɪəl]
adj. 忠诚的，忠心的

blow it
搞砸

curve [kɜːv]
n. 曲线；弯曲

shunt [ʃʌnt]
vi. 转轨；转向一边

return rate
回报率，退货率

具和电子产品。网车集团公司是一家日用杂货网上销售公司，它已经和美国贝克特尔工程建筑项目管理公司签订了一份 10 亿美元的订单，委托该公司为自己在美国的 26 个城市建造大型仓库。其他电子产品销售商，如电子玩具公司和巴恩斯诺布尔图书公司也都在兴建大型仓储项目。

安德生咨询公司电子商务部的副主任斯蒂夫·约翰逊说，这种投资对电子商务公司来说是必要的，只有这样，才能赢得大批忠实顾客。"对于这些公司来说，赢得顾客所花的成本是很高的，要盈利的话，你就必须要有大批回头客，"他说，"只要顾客有了一次不愉快的经历，你这单生意就永远搞砸了。"网络公司在试图掌控货运和仓储业务的同时，要学习的东西实在是多。将图书和光盘送进仓库并不麻烦，但像玩具、电子产品这些体积大，而且尺寸也各异的东西，就要困难得多。再者，诸如服装之类的商品，顾客退货率可高达 30%，处理好这类商品是颇为棘手的事情。

Learning Objectives 【学习目标】

- To understand the concept of warehousing.
- To identify various types of warehouse.
- To examine the trade-offs in warehousing layout.
- To learn the warehousing operation process.

Key Terms 【关键词】

warehousing	仓储	private warehouse	私有仓库
warehouse	仓库	public warehouse	公共仓库
warehouse layout	仓库布局	contract warehouse	合同仓库
automation	自动化	mechanization	机械化

Part 1　Introduction of Warehousing　仓储的概述

1. Definition of Warehousing

Warehousing has been defined as the part of logistics systems that store products (raw materials, parts, goods-in-process, finished goods) from points of origin to points of consumption. Warehousing can be provided by either warehouses or distribution centers. Warehouses **emphasize** the storage of products and their primary purpose is to maximize usage of available storage space. In contrast, distribution centers emphasize the rapid movement of products through a facility, and thus attempt to maximize **throughput** (the amount of product entering and leaving a facility in a given time period).

emphasize
['emfəsaɪz]
vt. 强调，着重

throughput
['θru:put]
n. 生产量，生产能力

1. 仓储的定义

仓储是物流系统的一部分，商品(包括原材料、零配件、在制品和产成品等)从原始起点到消费终点之间的存储就是仓储。仓储功能可以由仓库或配送中心提供。仓库强调货物的存储，其主要目标是存储空间的最大化使用。相反，配送中心强调的是货物在物流场所内的快速移动，以实现吞吐量(一定时期内进入和离开物流场所的货物数量)最大化。

2. Types of Warehouses

- Private warehouse

This type of warehouses are owned or occupied on a long-term **lease** by the firm using them. Private warehouses provide more control since the enterprise has absolute decision-making authority over all activities in the warehouse. The control facilitates the ability to integrate warehouse operations with the rest of the firm's internal logistics process. But the private warehouse is also characterized by some **drawbacks**, including high fixed cost of private storage and the necessity of having high and steady demand volumes. The largest users of private warehouses are **retail chain** stores. They handle large volumes of products on a regular basis. Manufacturing firms also utilize private warehouses.

- Public warehouse

The public warehouse is essentially space that can be leased to solve short-term distribution needs. Public warehouses offer more flexibility for the users since it requires no **capital** investment on user's part. Retailers that operate their own private warehouses may occasionally seek additional storage space if their facilities have reached capacity limit, or if they are making a special, large purchase of products. Public warehouses may also provide a number of specialized services that aren't available from other sources,

lease [li:s]
n. 租约；租期；租赁物；租赁权

drawback ['drɔ:bæk]
n. 缺点，不利条件

retail chain
连锁店；[贸易] 零售联营

capital ['kæpɪtəl]
adj. 重要的
n. 资金

2. 仓库的类型

- 私有仓库

这一类型的仓库可以是自己的，也可以是在长期租赁合同基础上供某一企业使用的。私有仓库的经营者对仓库业务有绝对的决策权，所以更易于对经营活动进行控制。这样仓储活动就能和企业内部其他的物流活动整合起来。但私有仓库也有一些缺点，包括私人仓储的固定成本高，并只有在需求量高且稳定的情况下才有利可图。私有仓库最大的使用者是连锁零售企业，因为他们依照常规需要处置大量的货物。制造企业也使用私有仓库。

- 公共仓库

公共仓库通过出租所需场地的方式为短期的商品存储提供服务。使用公共仓库具有更强的灵活性，因为使用者不需要投入大量资金。即使是拥有私有仓库的零售商在某些情况下也会租用公共仓库，比如当他们的仓库存储能力不足，或他们在进行特殊的大批量的采购时。公共仓库可能提供许多其他地方不能提供的专业服务，比如提供将较

such as value-added services in repackaging larger shipments into retail-size package, product assembly and product testing.

● Contract warehouse

For many years, organizations had two choices with respect to warehouse—public and private. But more recently, the contract warehouse (also referred to as third-party warehouse) has emerged as another warehouse alternative. The contract warehouse is a long-term, **mutually beneficial** arrangement which provides unique and specially tailored warehouse and logistics services for one customer. The contract warehouse is becoming a preferred choice for many organizations because it allows a company to focus on its **core competencies**, with warehouse provided by experts. The contract warehouse also tends to be more cost-effective than the private warehouse with almost the same degree of control, because key specifications can be included in the contracts.

大宗货物重新进行零售包装、产品组装和产品测试等增值服务。

● 合同仓库

多年来，企业对于仓库只有两种选择：使用公共仓库或使用私有仓库。但近年来，合同仓库(也称为第三方仓库)的出现使企业多了一个选择。合同仓库是一个长期的双方互惠协定，仓库设施的经营人对其客户提供独特的、专门的仓库和物流服务。很多企业愿意选择合同仓库的形式，因为让专业机构管理仓库的业务，他们就可以专注于发展自己的核心竞争力。合同仓库往往比私有仓库更经济，却能达到和私有仓库相近的控制程度，因为企业特定的要求都可以在合同中详细列明。

mutually beneficial
[贸易] 互利的；双赢的

core competencies
核心竞争力

Part 2 Warehousing Layout 仓储规划

Public warehouses are usually designed to handle a variety of items, while private warehouses are more specialized. Prior to designing a warehouse, the quantity and character of goods to be handled must be known.

The relative emphasis placed on the

公共仓库通常被规划为经营多种货物的仓库，而私有仓库多为专一型的仓库。规划仓库前，必须首先掌握待储存货物的数量和特性。

由于储存功能和配送

storage function and the distribution function affects space layout. A storage facility having low **rates of turnover** is laid out in a manner that maximizes utilization of the **cubic capacity** of the warehouse devoted to storage. A distribution-oriented facility would attempt to maximize "throughput" rather than storage.

Trade-offs must be made among space, labor, and mechanization. Before layout plans are made, each item that will be handled is studied in terms of its specific physical handling properties, the volume and regularity of movement, the frequency it is picked, and whether, compared to related items, it is "fast" or "slow" moving.

- **Horizontal** versus "high-rise" layout

The cubic capacity of a warehouse is a function of horizontal area times height. The relevant trade-off in utilizing a high-rise operation is between building costs, which declines on a cubic foot basis as one builds higher, and warehouse equipment costs, which increase.

- Order-picking versus stock-replenishing

Should workers who are picking outgoing orders and those who are restocking the warehouse work at the same time? Should they use the same **aisles**? How much space should be devoted to "active" or "live" stocks, which are stocks

---

rate of turnover
周转率

cubic capacity
立体容积

trade-off
['treɪdɒf,-ɔ:f]
n. 交换，交易；权衡；协定

horizontal
['hɒrɪ'zɒntəl]
adj. 水平的；地平线的

aisle [aɪl]
n. 通道，走道；侧廊

功能的相对侧重点不同，因此会影响仓库空间。一个转换率较低的储存仓库设备，主要依赖于最大化仓库的容积使用率。一个以配送为目标的仓库，将尽可能地最大化它的货物"吞吐量"，而不是存储量。

空间、劳动力和机械设施之间，必须权衡取舍。设计规划仓库之前，每个有待处理的项目都要根据它的特定物理处理性能进行分析研究，如：体积和运动规律、其被拣选的频率以及与相关项目相比是"快"还是"慢"。

- 水平布局与高层布局的对比

一个仓库的立方容量，是横向平面面积乘以高度的一个函数。利用高层运作需要平衡建设成本与仓储设备成本，其中建设成本随着立方英尺的增加而降低，而仓储设备成本则相应增加。

- 拣货与补货

工人可以同时进行出库订单分拣和入库订单分拣吗？二者能共用一个通道吗？拣货者依据填好的订单进行拣货，要有多大的空间才可以使库存"活跃"或"灵活"？对于这些等待

the order pickers pick from the fill orders? How much space is devoted to "reserve" stocks, which are stocks awaiting assignment to the active stock areas. If too much space is devoted to active stocks, the **bins** are larger and the order picker's travel time from bin to bin is increased. If the bins are smaller, the active stocks must be replenished from the reserve stock more frequently.

bin [bɪn]
n. 箱子，容器

- Two-dock versus single-dock layout

Conventional warehouses have the receiving dock on one end, the shipping dock on the other end, and goods move through between them. An **alternative** uses one dock that receives in the morning and ships out in the afternoon. Viewed from the top, the goods move in a U-shaped rather than a straight configuration. This reduces the space devoted to loading docks but requires carriers to pick up and deliver at more specific time.

alternative
[ɔːlˈtɜːnətɪv]
n. 可供选择(的事物)
adj. 两者(或两者以上)选择其一的；供替代的

- Space devoted to aisles versus space devoted to racks

As aisle space increases, storage capacity decreases. Wider aisles make it easier to operate mechanical equipment, but they increase travel distance within the facility.

- Labor-intensive versus highly mechanized

As labor costs increase, many warehouses place an increasing **reliance on** equipment to perform tasks that had once

reliance on
依靠；信赖

分配到活跃库存存放地的库存，要有多大空间能够提供给"储备"库存？如果太多空间是专门为活跃库存而设的，则存储位较大，并且增加了拣货者从一个储位向另一个储位移动的时间。如果储位较小，活跃库存必须频繁地从储备库存中进行补货。

- 两个船坞与单船坞布局的规划

传统仓库有一端是接收码头，另一端是运出码头，货物移动于它们之间。另一种是只使用一个船坞，早上接收，下午运出。从上往下看，货物移动呈现 U 形，而不是直线结构。单船坞降低了装货码头的规模，但要求承运人必须在非常特定时间里提货和送货。

- 过道与货架两者空间的比较

由于过道空间加大，储存容量减小。过道宽敞，易于操作机械设备，但它们增加了设施间的距离。

- 劳动力密集与高度机械化

由于劳动力成本不断地增加，许多仓库越来越依赖于设备来完成原来人工

been performed manually. Union Carbide has a 12-million cubic foot warehouse in West Virginia that can hold 64000 drums of chemicals. Two people (one of whom is a computer programmer) can handle the entire warehouse.

- Picker to part or part to picker

Some sophisticated systems for handling small parts are designed so that the **trays** with specific, wanted parts can be programmed to appear in front of the individual "picking" orders. This differs from the older system of having the picker seek out the part at the location where it was stored. The search time, component of total order picking time, is significantly reduced since the correct pick location is automatically presented to the order picker.

tray [treɪ]
n. 托盘

执行的任务。美国西弗吉尼亚州的 Union Carbide 有一个 12 万立方英尺的仓库，可容纳 64000 桶化学品，只需要两个人(其中一个人是电脑程序员)就可以管理整个仓库。

- 人到零件或零件到人

为了处理小型零部件，设计一些精密系统，通过编程，每张"拣货订单"所对应具体的、需要的零部件的情况，便可以出现在显示器上。这不同于从存放地点查找零部件的旧方法。搜索时间、总的拣货时间大幅减少，这是因为正确的拣货地点是自动呈现在拣货人面前的。

Part 3　Warehousing Operation Process　仓储运作流程

Warehousing operation process is as follows.

- Goods inwards

This includes the physical unloading of incoming transport, checking, recording of receipts, and deciding where the received goods are to be put away in the warehouse. It can also include such activities as **unpacking** and repackaging, quality control checks and temporary **quarantine** storage for goods awaiting clearance by quality control.

unpacking
[ˌʌnˈpækɪŋ]
n. 开包；取出货物

quarantine
[ˈkwɒrəntiːn]
vi. 实行隔离
n. 隔离；检疫

仓储操作有以下运作流程。

- 进货

这个过程包括卸货搬运、核对验收、记录接收和指定货物的存放场地，还包括一些其他活动，比如：拆包和重新包装、质量检验、暂时隔离储存等待检验通关的货物。

- Reserve storage

Reserve or backup storage, which is the largest space user in many warehouses, holds **the bulk of** warehouse stock in identifiable locations. Goods are moved to reserve storage from goods inwards, and the locations communicated to the warehouse information system.

- Replenishment

This is the movement of goods in larger than order quantities, for a whole pallet at a time from reserve storage to order picking to ensure that order picking locations do not become empty. Maintaining stock availability for order picking is important for example, locations achieving high levels of order fill.

- Order picking

Goods are selected from order picking stock in the required quantities and at the required time to meet customer orders. Picking often involves break bulk operation, for example, goods are received from suppliers in a whole pallet quantities, but are ordered by customers in less than a pallet quantities. However, if a particular product is required in a sufficiently large quantity, for example a whole pallet load, it is picked directly from reserve storage. Order picking is important for achieving high-level customer service; it traditionally does take a high **proportion** of the total warehouse staff complement and is expensive. The good design and management

reserve
[rɪ'zɜ:v]
n. 储备，储存
v. 保留

the bulk of
大多数，大部分

proportion
[prə'pɔ:ʃ(ə)n]
n. 比例；部分；面积

- 保留存储仓位

保留仓位或备用仓位占据了多数仓库的大部分空间，大多数货物存储在可识别的仓位上。这些先前所进的货物及其位置也相应地输入到仓库的信息系统中。

- 补货

搬运的货物比订单需求的数量多。例如货物从存储区向拣选区转移的过程中，托盘每次都会装满，以保证拣选区不会为空。要想高水平地完成订单，维持足够的拣选货物是非常重要的。

- 拣选

我们需要在所需时间内拣选足够数量的货物以满足顾客的订单需求。拣选一般伴随着散装货的操作过程，例如货物从供应商处取回时是一个托盘的数量，而顾客所需数量少于一个托盘。但是，如果顾客大量地需求某类货物，例如整个托盘的货物，就可以直接从存储仓位中拣选。要想获得较高的顾客服务水平，拣选这一步是非常重要的，它要用到仓库的大部分工作人员，并且成本也比较高。良好的拣选系统设计和管理及运行对有效的仓储运作

of picking systems and operations are consequently vital to effective warehouse performance.

- Secondary sortation

For small-size order, it is sometimes appropriate to **batch** numbers of orders together and treat them as "one" order for picking purposes. In this case, the picked batch will have to be sorted down to individual orders: secondary sortation, before dispatched.

- Sortation

In some **circumstances**, the use of information technology means that the ultimate destinations of a significant proportion of the goods coming into a warehouse are known. Recent developments have therefore used this facility to enable goods coming into a warehouse to be sorted into specific customer orders immediately on arrival, sometimes, with high-speed sortation conveyors. The goods then go directly to order **collation**. This approach has been used for some years in cross docking operations for grocery produce by major supermarkets.

- Collation

After picking, goods are brought together and consolidated as a completed order ready for **dispatch** to customers. This can involve packing into dispatch outer cases and cartons, labeling operations and stretch and **shrink wrapping** for load protector and stability.

batch
[bætʃ]
n. 一批，一组
vt. 分批处理

circumstance
['sɜːkəmstəns]
n. 环境，情况；事件；境遇

collation
[kɒ'leɪʃən]
n. 校对

dispatch
[dɪs'pætʃ]
vt. 派遣；发送
n. 派遣；发送

shrink wrapping
紧缩包装，收缩包装；热塑收缩包装

至关重要。

- 二次分货

对于数量少的订单，可以把它们结合在一起，作为"一个"订单进行拣选。在这种情况下，发货前拣选完的大订单还要再分为原来的小订单，也就是二次分货。

- 分货

在某些环境下，信息技术的应用意味着我们可以知道进入仓库的大部分货物最终的目的地。根据顾客订单，使用高速分拣传送带对进入仓库的货物进行分类，然后把这些货物直接送到订单核对环节。这种方法早在几年前就已经应用到大型超市的食品类商品的交叉收货环节中。

- 核对

在拣选完以后，把货物集中在一起拼装成一个完整的订单准备发货。这个过程涉及的活动有：打包、贴标签，为了保护和稳固货物还要利用到伸缩包装。

- Dispatch

Picked, collated and packed goods are assembled for loading to outbound vehicles and onward dispatch to the next "mode" in the supply chain intermediate distribution center, next transport vehicle such as air or ship, or direct to final customers.

The above list indicates the principal activities found in warehousing operations. In addition, there can be a range of **subsidiary** activities such as packaging material stores, sub assembly and packing areas, truck battery charging areas, equipment maintenance shops, offices and amenities, and in some cases services to support specific product environment such as chill or frozen goods stores.

subsidiary
[səb'sɪdɪərɪ]
adj. 附属的；辅助的

- 发货

拣选、复核、打包完的货物被装上货车发送到供应链中的另一个"节点"即中间配送中心，下一个运输工具可能是飞机、轮船或直接送到顾客手中。

以上所列的是仓储运作的主要活动，另外，还有很多辅助活动，比如包装材料的储存、局部装配、设立包装区、卡车充电区、设备维修车间、办公室以及便利设施等。有些仓库还为某类货物设立专门的储存环境，比如冷藏或冷冻货物的储存。

Part 4   Specimen Letters 信函范例

Instructions for Goods Storage

June 6, 2019
Dear Mr. Han,

Instructions for Goods Storage (Order No.12402)

With reference to the above order of 1000 wineglasses, we would like to give you the special storage and delivery instructions.

As the goods are fragile, please handle with care and do not stack them up for storage.

Your extra care of the goods is highly appreciated.

仓储要求

韩先生：

仓储要求(订单编号：12402)

就以上 1000 件酒杯订单，本公司现提供有关储存及运送的指示。

由于该批货品易碎，存放时请勿把木箱叠起，运送时亦须小心轻放。

感谢贵公司仓储职员加倍注意以上储存的方法。

Yours sincerely, Tianming Liu(Ms.) Manager	经理 刘天明 2019 年 6 月 6 日

Summary 本章小结

Warehousing has been defined as the part of logistics systems that store products (raw materials, parts, goods-in-process, finished goods) from points of origin to points of consumption. This chapter provides an overview of warehousing, warehousing layout and warehousing operation process. Besides, the letter of goods storage is also detailed.

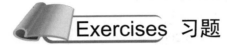

Exercises 习题

Questions for Review 复习题

1. What is the warehousing?
2. What are the main characteristics of private warehouses, public warehouses and contract warehouses?
3. What is the warehousing operation process?
4. What are the fundamental principles for warehousing layout?
5. What is the order picking?

True or False 判断对错

1. Warehouse rental represents a very significant proportion of total warehouse cost.
2. The size of warehouses is determined by the needs of the customer groups, such as their inventory level planning.
3. Public warehouses are usually designed to handle a variety of items, while private warehouses are more specialized.
4. Warehouse emphasizes the rapid movement of products through a facility and maximize throughput.
5. Secondary sortation takes a high proportion of the total warehouse staff complement.

Topic for Discussion 讨论话题

Public warehouses offer more flexibility for users since it requires no capital investment on users' part. Do you agree that manufactories should use public warehouses instead of owning their private warehouses?

Logistics English Dialogue 物流英语对话

Storage Management Agency

(A: a clerk who is responsible for receiving customers; B: a young businessman who is enquiring about storage.)

A: Good morning, sir. Can I help you?

B: Good morning, I want to know whether you handle warehouse storage.

A: Sure, what kind of goods do you want us to store?

B: A set of textiles and a set of glass craftworks.

A: And how many do you need to store?

B: We have 500 pieces of textiles and 200 pieces of glass craftworks.

A: How long do you intend us to store them for you? Do you want us to offer delivery/shipment as well?

B: Textiles for a month, and glass craftworks for 20 days. And I need your delivery/shipment service, too. How much do you charge? Would you please show me around the warehouse?

(The receptionist shows the warehouse to the customer on computer.)

A: Of course. You can bring forward your storage request, and we will try to meet your needs. You see, we manage the goods through the computer's data system.

B: (Pointing at the numbers on the layout of the warehouse on the computer) Excuse me, what are the numbers?

A: They are serial numbers referring to the goods stored. For example, No. 3-12-6-8 means that the eighth case of the sixth layer of the twelfth shelfis in the third warehouse.

B: Oh, I see. Thanks. I am impressed with the overall management level of the warehouse, and I will come back very soon.

A: Thank you. Welcome again. Bye bye.

B: Bye.

Case Study 案例分析题

Cross Docks in Warehouses

If an arriving item has already been requested by a customer, there is no need to store it as anticipation inventory; instead, the item can move directly from receiving to shipping, without intermediate storage and retrieval. Thus the item can move much more quickly through the facility and the most costly part of warehouse labor can be avoided. In a high-volume cross dock, the turnover times may be measured in hours. To support this velocity of movement, a cross dock may be nothing more than a slab of concrete with a roof and walls punctuated with doors for trailers. Freight is pulled off arriving trailers, sorted and loaded onto departing trailers without intermediate storage.

There is little or no storage provided in a cross dock because items do not stay long enough; but there is generally a lot of material-handling equipment, such as forklifts and pallet jacks, to move freight. Labor is frequently the main cost and it is devoted to unloading incoming trailers, moving the freight to the appropriate outgoing trailers, and loading. Consequently, the issues within a cross dock are those of material-handling and product flow rather than location and retrieval. Why is cross-docking becoming popular with retailers?

Because of its impact on costs and customer service, cross-docking is becoming popular, especially with retailers. For example, approximately 75 percent of food distribution involves the cross-docking of products from suppliers to retail food stores. The biggest impact of a cross dock is on reducing transportation costs. This can be achieved by consolidating multiple shipments so that full truck loads can be sent. Home Depot is a major retailer and the largest user of Less-than-Truck-Load (LTL) shipping in North America. Nowadays, LTL costs about twice the cost of Truck Load (TL) shipping, so there is a strong incentive to fill trailers. Home Depot has begun doing this by having vendors ship full trailers to its cross dock (the trailers are full because they hold products for many stores). At the cross dock, the products are sorted out for individual stores and consolidated with products from other vendors bound for the same store. The result is that each store has enough freight and a few close neighbors generate a full truck load from the cross dock. The result can be considerable savings. Additional benefits include less inventory (because all products flow right through) and less labor (because products do not have to be put away and later retrieved).

Discussion: What are the benefits from cross docks in warehouses?

Chapter 7

Inventory Management
库存管理

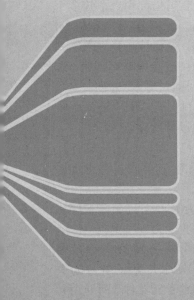

Seagate VMI Mode
希捷 VMI 库存模式

With revenue of 8 billion US dollars, Seagate is the biggest global manufacturer of hard disk drives. With a shipment volume of 100 million sets hard disk drives per annum, Seagate sees a daily consumption of 90 million parts and components. Its products are sold everywhere around the world and extensively applied in various fields such as PCs, **laptops**, game machines, TV sets, digital cameras, and automobiles. Seagate's application of the VMI/SMI mode mainly corresponds to its **demand-driven** supply chain strategy, which involves four aspects.

(1) To eliminate the **surplus** stocks at every stage of the supply chain.

(2) To reduce the stock rotation period.

(3) To provide better customer service.

(4) To strengthen reaction to demand variations.

Seagate's VMI/SMI solutions focus key manufacturing strategy on only competitive techniques and components, whereas the supply of general components and assembly is undertaken by its suppliers.

Seagate faces challenges: products

laptop
['læptɒp]
n. 膝上型轻便电脑

demand-driven
adj. [计] 需求驱动的

surplus
['sɜːplʌs, -pləs]
adj. 剩余的；过剩的

希捷公司是全球最大的磁盘驱动器制造商，年收入达到 80 亿美元。希捷每年硬盘驱动器的出货量高达 1 亿台，每天要消耗 9000 万个零部件，产品销售到全球各地，被广泛应用到 PC、笔记本电脑、游戏机、电视机、数码相机和汽车等多个领域。希捷应用 VMI/SMI 模式，主要是与其需求驱动型的供应链策略相呼应，它的目标包括四个方面。

(1) 消除供应链每个阶段的过量库存。

(2) 缩短库存周转时间。

(3) 向客户提供更优质的服务。

(4) 增强对于需求变化的应变能力。

希捷公司的制造策略只是关注具有竞争力的关键技术和元器件，而通用元器件和装配等由其供应商承担。

希捷公司所面临的挑战是产品的功能不断提升，

Chapter 7 Inventory Management
库存管理

keep **upgrading** its functions and their lifecycle is getting shorter. New products are launched every week. Consequently, its customers' requirements keep changing faster and faster, whereas they still highly expect Seagate to make timely and accurate shipment.

In order to solve this problem, Seagate has **shifted** to the demand-driven supply chain strategy and launched efficient VMI/SMI project, in which Seagate sets up two VMI/SMI centers: one between Seagate and its customers, known as the JIT centre, is managed by Seagate itself; the other between Seagate and its suppliers is outsourced to a third-party logistics providers.

Because of the real-time transfer of information throughout the whole supply chain, Seagate can schedule its production totally on the basis of customer orders, hence creating more flexibility for manufacturing and extensively reducing the stock level.

Before making improvement to the work flow process, it took a 30-day replenishment period for Seagate. Having redesigned the process and realized automated operation, the 30-day replenishment period is reduced by half. Not only can the supply chain team capture information **swiftly**, **labour cost** is also reduced substantially. Aided by the automated process, Seagate has reduced its labour cost and related costs to below 50%.

upgrade ['ʌpgreɪd]
vt. 升级；提高；改善

shift [ʃɪft]
vi. 移动；转变；转换

swiftly ['swɪftlɪ]
adv. 很快地；敏捷地；即刻
labour cost
人工成本

产品的生命周期越来越短，每周都有新产品推出。结果希捷客户的需求变化越来越快，但是他们对希捷及时和准确的出货仍然抱有较高的期望。

为解决该问题，希捷公司的供应链策略转向需求驱动型，并推行高效率的VMI/SMI项目。在这条供应链中，希捷设立了两个VMI/SMI中心，一个设在希捷与客户之间，称为JIT中心，由希捷自己负责管理；另一个设在希捷与其供应商之间，外包给第三方物流提供商管理。

由于信息在整个供应链中的实时传递，希捷可以完全根据客户的订单安排生产，从而为生产制造带来更多弹性，并大幅减少库存量。

在流程改善之前，希捷需要30天的补货周期。重新设计流程和实现运作自动化之后，30天的补货周期减少了一半，供应链团队不仅可以很快获得信息，而且减少了大量人工成本。希捷借助自动化流程，将人力和相关成本减少到50%以下。

专栏 7-1 希捷

希捷公司成立于1979年，现为全球最大的硬盘、磁盘和读写磁头制造商。希捷在设计、制造和销售硬盘领域居全球领先地位，提供用于企业、台式电脑、移动设备和消费电子的产品。自创建以来，希捷一直是存储设备技术领域的领导者，它是数字世界的心脏，并将继续站在创新前沿。希捷提出的云计算存储解决方案全球领先，结合统一存储构架来提供更加灵活、更低成本的计算。统一存储作为企业存储的领导者，已经发展了30多年，能够提供强劲而简单的企业级存储解决方案。

Learning Objectives【学习目标】

- To understand the definition of inventory.
- To learn contemporary approaches of inventory management.
- To learn the methods of collaborative inventory replenishment.

Key Terms 【关键词】

inventory management	库存管理	economies of scale	规模经济效益
ABC classification	ABC 分类	collaborative inventory replenishment	联合库存补充
quick response	快速响应	profile replenishment	系列补货

Part 1　Definition of Inventory Management 库存管理的定义

Inventory management is the **branch** of business management concerned with the planning and controlling of inventories. Inventory management is required at different locations within a facility or within multiple locations of a supply network to protect the regular and planned course of production against the random **disturbance** of running out of materials or goods.

branch
[brɑːntʃ, bræntʃ]
n. 树枝，分枝；分部；支流

disturbance
[dɪˈstɜːbəns]
n. 干扰；骚乱

库存管理是企业管理的一个分支，涉及存货的计划与控制。库存管理有必要在同一个工厂的不同地点或同一个供应网络的多个地点进行，以防止货物和物资供应不足而干扰正常的和计划的生产进程。

不同的功能部门具有

Chapter 7 Inventory Management
库存管理

Different organizational functions can have different inventory management objectives. Marketing, for example, tends to ensure that **sufficient** inventory is available for customer demand in order to avoid potential stockout situations, which translates into higher inventory level. Alternatively, the finance group generally seeks to minimize the costs associated with holding inventory, which translates into lower inventory level.

The scope of inventory management concerns the fine lines at replenishment lead time, carrying costs of inventory, asset management, inventory forecasting, inventory valuation, inventory **visibility**, future inventory price forecasting, physical inventory, available physical space for inventory, quality management, replenishment, returns and defective goods and demand forecasting.

● The reasons for keeping inventory

There are three basic reasons for keeping an inventory.

(1) Time

The time lags presented in the supply chain, from suppliers to users at every stage, requires that you maintain certain amount of inventory to use in this "**lead time**".

(2) Uncertainty

Inventories are maintained as buffers to meet uncertainties in demand, supply and movements of goods.

---

sufficient [sə'fɪʃənt] adj. 足够的；充分的

visibility [ˌvɪzɪ'bɪlətɪ] n. 能见度，可见性

lead time n. 提前期；订货至交货的时间

不同的库存管理目标。例如，市场营销部门往往要确保有足够的库存以满足客户未来的需求，避免潜在缺货的情况，这意味着保持更高的库存水平。相反地，财务部门通常要减少持有库存，降低其所花费的成本，这就要求保持较低的库存水平。

库存管理的范围涉及补货前置期的细微差别、库存持有成本、资产管理、库存预测、库存估价、库存可见性、未来库存品价格预测、实地盘存、存货可用的空间、质量管理、补货、退货和次品以及需求预测。

● 持有库存的原因

持有库存有三个基本原因。

(1) 时间

客户每一个阶段都存在时间滞后，要求在这个"前置期"(订货与交货之间相隔的时间)有一定的库存量可供使用。

(2) 不确定性

库存作为缓冲区，以应付需求、供应和货物流动的不确定性。

(3) Economies of scale

Ideal condition of "one unit at a time at a place where a user needs it, when he needs it" principle tends to incur lots of costs in terms of logistics. So bulk buying, movement and storing brings in economies of scale, and thus inventory.

All these stock reasons can apply to any owner or product stage.

- Reasons against inventory

Critics have challenged the holding of inventories along several lines. First, inventories are considered wasteful. They absorb capital that might otherwise be put to better use, such as to improve **productivity** or competitiveness. Second, they can mask quality problems. Finally, excessive inventories may compensate for **deficiencies** in basic design of a logistic system, but will at last result in higher necessary total logistics cost.

productivity
[ˌprədʌkˈtɪvətɪ, ˌprəʊ-]
n. 生产力；生产率；生产能力

deficiency
[dɪˈfɪʃənsɪ]
n. 缺乏；不足；缺点；缺陷

(3) 规模经济效益

以"在客户需要的某个时间地点提供某批货物"为原则的理想条件往往会产生许多物流方面的费用。因此，大宗购买、运输和储存带来了规模经济效益，也带来了库存。

所有这些持有库存的原因适用于任何货主及产品(生产和流通的)任何阶段。

- 反对库存的原因

反对者从几个方面质疑持有库存。首先，库存被看作是浪费。库存占用过多资金，这些资金可能有更好的用处，如用于提高生产力和竞争力。其次，库存会掩盖质量问题。最后，过多的库存可能会掩盖在物流系统的基本设计缺陷，但最终会导致必要的总成本过高。

Part 2 ABC Classification ABC 分类

The objective of ABC classification is to focus and refine inventory management efforts. ABC classification, which is also called product/market classification, groups products, markets, or customers with similar characteristics to facilitate inventory management. The classification process recognizes that not all products and markets have the same characteristics or degree of importance, different products and markets have their own particulars. Sound inventory management requires that classification be consistent with enterprise strategy and service objectives.

Classification can be based on a variety of measures. The most common are sales, profit contribution, inventory value, usage rate, and nature of the item. The typical classification process sequences products or markets so that entries with similar characteristics are grouped together. Classification by sales volume is one of the oldest methods used to establish selective inventory policies. For most marketing or logistics applications, a small percentage of the **entities** account for a large percentage of the volume. This operationalization is often called the 80/20 rule or Pareto's law. The 80/20 rule, which is based on **widespread** observations, states that for a

entity ['entɪtɪ]
n. 实体；存在；本质

widespread ['waɪdspred; -'spred]
adj. 普遍的，广泛的；分布广的

ABC 分类的目的是集中和优化库存管理，通常也称为产品/市场分类。在分类时，需要对具有相同特点的产品、市场和客户进行分组。此外，还要注意一点，产品和市场并不一定都具有相同的特点和同等的重要性，不同的产品和市场往往有其独特之处。完善的库存管理要确保分类工作与企业的战略和服务目标相一致。

分类指标很多，最常见的指标有销售额、利润贡献率、库存价值、利用率以及产品的特点。在一般的分类过程中，企业通常对产品和市场进行排序。这样，具有相同特征的事物就会被分在一组。利用销售额来进行分类是企业制定库存策略时采用的最传统的方法之一。对于大多数市场营销或者物流运作而言，一小部分产品的销售量往往占总销售量的绝大部分。这通常称为 80/20 法则或者帕累托法则。80/20 法则是在大量的实践观察的基础上得出的，它指出一个企业 20%的产

typical enterprise 80 percent of the sales volume is typically accounted for by 20 percent of the products. A corollary to the rule is that 80 percent of enterprise sales is accounted for by 20 percent of the customers. The reverse perspective of the rule would state that the remaining 20 percent of sales is obtained from 80 percent of the products, customers, etc. In general terms, the 80/20 rule implies that a majority of sales results from a relatively few products or customers.

Once items are classified or grouped, it is common to label each category with a character or description. High-volume, fast-moving products are often described as A items. The **moderate** volume items are termed B items, and the low-volume or slow movers are known as C items. These character labels indicate why this process is often termed ABC analysis. While fine-line classification often uses three categories, some firms use four or five categories to further refine classifications. Grouping of similar products not only facilitates management processes but also help establish focused inventory strategies for specific product segments. For example, high-volume or fast-moving products are typically targeted for higher service level. This often requires that fast-moving items have relatively more safety stock. **Conversely**, to reduce overall

moderate
['mɒd(ə)rət]
*adj.*适度的，中等的；有节制的

conversely
['kɒnvɜːslɪ]
adv. 相反地

品占据了总销售额的80%。这一法则的推论是20%的客户为企业贡献了总销售额的80%。换个角度来说，也就是剩余的80%的产品、客户对总销售额只作出了20%的贡献。综上所述，80/20法则意味着销售额的大部分来自相对较少的产品和客户。

一旦完成产品的分类或分组，我们通常会为每一类产品进行标注。畅销的、流通速度较快的产品通常会被标记为A类，中等的被标记为B类，滞销的、流通速度较慢的产品，则被标记为C类。正是因为这些字母标记，所以这种方法才被称为ABC分类法。ABC分类法通常使用3种不同的类别，也有一些企业使用4~5个类别，对产品做出进一步的细分。将同种性质的产品进行归类，既简化了产品的管理过程，同时也有助于企业有针对性地为产品制定合适的库存策略。例如，畅销的、流通速度较快的产品通常要求高质量的服务，因此企业就可以适当增加这类产品的安全库存量。相反

Chapter 7 Inventory Management
库存管理

inventory level, slower-moving items may be allowed relatively less safety stock, resulting in lower service level.

In special situations, classification systems may be based on multiple factors. For example, item gross margin and importance to customers can be weighted to develop a combined index instead of simply using sales volume. The weighted rank would then group items that have similar **profitability** and importance. The inventory policy, including safety stock levels, is then established using the weighted rank.

The classification array defines product or market groups to be assigned similar inventory strategies. The use of item groups facilitates the **identification** and specification of inventory strategies without requiring tedious development of individual item strategies. It is much easier to track and manage 3 to 10 groups instead of hundreds of individual items.

profitability
[ˌprɒfɪtə'bɪlətɪ]
n. 赢利能力；收益性；实用性

identification
[aɪˌdentɪfɪ'keɪʃ(ə)n]
n. 鉴定，识别；认同；身份证明

地，为了减少库存总量，企业可以减少流通速度较慢产品的安全库存，酌情降低该类产品服务水平。

在某些特殊情况下，分类系统还需要综合考虑多种因素的影响。例如，企业可以将产品的总利润以及对客户的重要性进行加权，得到一个综合指标，然后利用该指标对产品进行分类，来代替仅仅只使用销售额这一种指标的分类方法。使用上述加权分类法，企业就能将利润相似、重要性相近的产品归为一类。随后，在加权分类的基础上，企业可以有针对性地制定出库存策略，包括安全库存量。

分类法明确了产品或市场以相似库存策略划分的分组。分组后，企业不再需要对数量众多的单个产品开发出多种库存策略，从而简化了制定库存策略的过程。显而易见的是，对3～10组产品进行跟踪和管理远远比对上百种单独的产品进行跟踪和管理要容易得多。

Part 3   Collaborative Inventory Replenishment 联合库存补充

Several collaborative **initiatives** focus only on inventory replenishment. Replenishment programs are designed to streamline the flow of goods within the supply chain. There are several specific techniques for collaborative replenishment, all of which build on supply chain relationships to rapidly replenish inventory on the basis of joint planning or actual sales experience. The intent is to reduce reliance on forecasting when and where inventory will need to be positioned to demand on a just-in-time basis. Effective collaborative replenishment programs require extensive cooperation and information sharing among supply chain partners. Specific techniques for **collaborative** inventory replenishment are quick response, vendor-managed inventory, and profile replenishment.

1. Quick Response

A technology-driven cooperative effort between retailers and suppliers to improve inventory **velocity** while providing merchandise supply closely matched to consumers' buying patterns is quick response (QR). QR is implemented by sharing retail sales for specific products among supply chain

initiative
[ɪˈnɪʃɪətɪv; -ʃə-]
n. 主动权；首创精神

collaborative
[kəˈlæbəretɪv]
adj. 合作的，协作的

velocity
[vɪˈlɒsɪtɪ]
n. [力] 速率；迅速；周转率

不少企业在进行合作时，仅仅将注意力放在了库存的补充上。设计补货程序有助于提高供应链中物流运作的效率。不少特定的方法都能够实现联合补货。这些方法都是以实际的销售经验和协同计划为基础的，充分利用了供应链成员之间的合作关系，以实现快速补货。联合补货的目的是减少企业对预测的依赖。为了实现 JIT 供货，预测常常要对需求进行估计，从而确定需要库存的时间和地点。有效的联合补货计划，需要供应链的所有参与者之间开展广泛的合作，并且实现信息共享。实现联合补货的特定方法包括快速响应、供应商管理库存和系列补货。

1. 快速响应

当零售商向客户提供某种商品，同时为了尽可能与客户的购买方式达成一致时，零售商和供应商会同技术驱动而进行合作以便提高供货速度，这就是快速响应(QR)。在供应链的成员之间共享特定产品的销售信息，是实现 QR 的基础，从而有利于在任何时

participants to facilitate right product assortment availability when and where it is required. Instead of operating on a order cycle for 15 to 30 days, QR arrangements can replenish retail inventories in six days or less. Continuous information exchange regarding availability and delivery reduces uncertainty for the total supply chain and creates the opportunity for maximum flexibility. With fast, dependable order response, inventory can be committed as required, resulting in increased **turnover** and improved availability. WalMart's system is a prime example of the power of sharing sales to facilitate QR.

2. Vendor-Managed Inventory

In Chapter 2 vendor-managed inventory (VMI) was introduced and discussed, which is a modification of quick response that eliminates the need for replenishment orders. The goal is to establish so flexible and efficient a supply chain arrangement that retail inventory is continuously replenished. The **distinguishing** factor between QR and VMI is who takes responsibility for setting target inventory levels and making restocking decisions. In QR, the retailer determines target inventory level and makes the decisions. In VMI, the supplier **assumes** more responsibility and actually manages a category of

participant
[pɑːˈtɪsɪp(ə)nt]
n. 参与者；关系者

turnover
[ˈtɜːnəʊvə]
n. 营业额；流通量

distinguish
[dɪˈstɪŋɡwɪʃ]
adj. 有区别的

assume
[əˈsjuːm]
vt. 承担

间、任何地点都能够提供所需产品。例如，QR可以在6天甚至更短的时间内完成对零售商品的补货，而不是通常情况下的15~30天。如果合作双方能够持续地交换有关产品可用性以及交货等方面的信息，那么就可以大大减少供应链的不确定性，同时也可以提高企业的柔性，并有可能达到最高水平。快速、可靠的响应机制可以确保客户及时获得所需的库存，还可以提高库存周转率，提高产品的可用性。沃尔玛的系统就是应用QR的一个绝佳例证。

2. 供应商管理库存

我们在第2章中对供应商管理库存(VMI)探讨过。VMI是在对QR的进一步完善中发展起来的，它有效地减少了企业对补货的需求。VMI的目的在于建立一个灵活有效的供应链体系，从而不断地对零售库存进行补充。QR和VMI明显的区别在于，谁负责制定目标库存量和补货决策。在QR中，零售商确定目标库存量并且制定补货决策。而在VMI中，供应商则承担了更多责任，并且实际上是由供应商为零售商管理库存。当供应商获得了每日的销售量及仓库运

inventory for the retailer. By receiving daily transmission of retail sales or warehouse shipments, the supplier assumes responsibility for replenishing retail inventory in the required quantities, colors, sizes, and styles. The supplier commits to keeping the retailer in stock and to maintaining inventory velocity. In some situations, replenishment involves cross-docking or direct store delivery (DSD) designed to eliminate the need for warehousing between the supplier and retailer.

3. Profile Replenishment

Some manufacturers, wholesalers, and retailers are experimenting with an even more sophisticated collaboration known as profile replenishment (PR). The PR strategy extends QR and VMI by giving suppliers the right to anticipate future requirements according to their overall knowledge of a **merchandise** category. A category profile details the combination of sizes, colors, and associated products that usually sell in a particular type of retail outlet. Given PR responsibility, the supplier can simplify retailers' involvement by eliminating the need to track unit sales and inventory level for fast-moving products.

Many firms, particularly manufacturers, are using **DRP** and even APS logic to coordinate inventory planning with

merchandise ['mɜːtʃ(ə)ndaɪs; -z]
n. 商品；货物

DRP (distribution resource planning) *abbr.* 分销资源计划

输量等信息之后，它就要承担起责任，按照数量、颜色、大小和款式等方面的要求为零售商进行补货。供应商向零售商承诺不会发生缺货，并且要保证一定的供货速度。在某些情况下，补货过程涉及交叉运作或者直接向商店送货(DSD)，这些运作模式旨在避免供应商与零售商之间的仓储需求。

3. 系列补货

目前，一些制造商、批发商和零售商正在共同致力于一种更为复杂的合作方式。该方式被称为系列补货(PR)。PR决策是QR和VMI的扩展，它允许供应商根据其对各种产品系列的了解去对未来的需求进行预测。产品系列的特征包括产品的大小和颜色等信息，此外，产品系列还涉及在特定类型零售店中销售的相关产品，并对这些产品进行了详细说明，使用PR运作模式，供应商通过避免对快速流通商品的销售情况与库存水平的跟踪来简化零售商的参与。

许多企业，尤其是制造商，在与主要客户开展库存计划方面的合作时，使用了DRP

major customers. The manufacturers are extending their planning framework to include customer warehouses and, in some cases, their retail stores. Such integrated planning capabilities facilitate manufacturer coordination and management of customer inventories.

模式或 APS 技术。制造商正逐渐把客户的仓库纳入到其计划范围之内，有时甚至还会包括一些零售商店。这种集成的计划模式有利于制造商对客户的库存进行协调和管理。

Summary 本章小结

This chapter introduces the topic of inventory, which starts with the reason holding inventories and against inventories. It also introduces ABC classification to managing inventory. At last, collaborative inventory replenishment is discussed.

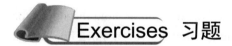

Exercises 习题

Questions for Review 复习题

1. What is the inventory?
2. Why should a manufactory keep inventory?
3. What are contemporary approaches of inventory management?
4. Why should a company classify its inventory items into an A, B and C class?

True or False 判断对错

1. Lead time is the time between placing a purchase order and actually receiving the goods ordered.
2. Safety stock refers to inventory that is needed to satisfy normal demand during the course of an order cycle.
3. "A" items approximately represent 85 percent of total inventory costs.
4. The JIT approach seeks to minimize inventory by reducing cycle stock.
5. Forecasting demand is an essential prerequisite for an effective stock control system.

Topic for Discussion 讨论话题

The JIT approach brings benefits to the manufacturers. They can have the required amount of materials arrive at the production location at the exact right time, and keep little even zero inventory. But that means the suppliers have to deliver their materials more often to meet this requirement. Do you agree JIT is an unfair practice for the suppliers?

Logistic English Dialogue 物流英语对话

(A, manager of a supermarket store, is discussing with B, manager of a local distributor, on the possibility of introducing VMI system in the store.)

A: I have a question for you concerning inventory management.

B: Yes, please.

A: We are holding stocks in our own warehouse. You know these tie up the capital and manpower. Can you assist us in designing a new inventory method?

B: With pleasure. I suppose vendor-managed inventory, or VMI, is the best approach for a medium sized store like yours.

A: What's VMI? Can you explain a bit?

B: In simple words, it means we, the distributor, hold the stocks for you, the retail store, and you can inform us whenever an item is below the safety stock line.

A: Sounds marvelous. Does it mean we no longer have to keep our own stocks?

B: No, you don't have to. We manage the inventory for you; you order items anytime you feel like it.

A: How do you guarantee fast delivery? You know if I order certain items in the morning, I want it to be on shelf in the afternoon.

B: No problem with that. We offer same-day delivery service to our customers.

A: What happens if I need an urgent item? Can you also make quick delivery in short notice?

B: For high-cost items, yes.

A: For example?

B: If you order home appliances from us, they can reach you in less than two hours.

A: I'm satisfied with that. In this case we will be operating zero inventory. And our inventory cost will be minimized.

B: That's the advantage of VMI.

A: By the way, if we have some unsold items, can we return them to you?

B: Sure. As VMI operators, we not only distribute goods to customers, but also receive customer returns when necessary. This is part of our business.

Chapter 7 Inventory Management
库存管理

Case Study 案例分析题

Managing Stock to Meet Customers' Needs

McDonald's is one of only a handful of brands that command instant recognition in virtually every country in the world. It has more than 30000 restaurants in over 119 countries, serving around 50 million people every day. One of the major challenges faced by McDonald's is managing stock. Stock management involves creating a balance between meeting customers' needs and minimizing waste.

As customers' taste change, McDonald's needs to increase the range of new products it offers, so the challenge of reducing waste becomes even greater. In the past, stock ordering was the responsibility of individual restaurant managers. They ordered stock using their local knowledge, as well as data on what the store sold the previous day, week and month. For example, if last week's sales figures showed they sold 100 units of coffee and net sales were rising at 10%, they would expect to sell 110 units this week. However, this was a simple method and involved no calculations to take into account of factors such as national promotions or school holidays. It took the Restaurant Manager a lot of time, leaving them less time to concentrate on delivering quality food, service and cleanliness in the restaurants. In 2004, McDonald's introduced a specialist central stock management function known as the Restaurant Supply Planning Department. This team communicates with restaurant managers on a regular basis to find out local events. The team builds these factors into the new planning and forecasting system (called Manugistics) to forecast the likely demand of finished menu items (e.g. Big Macs).

Types of stock:
- The raw materials are the ingredients that will go into producing the finished product. For McDonald's, these will include the buns, beef patties, paper cups, salad ingredients and packaging. These are delivered to the restaurants between 3 and 5 times a week. The raw materials arrive together on one lorry with three sections so that each product can be stored at a suitable temperature.
- Work-in-progress refers to stocks that are in the process of being made into finished product. A Big Mac consists of a bun, two beef patties, lettuce, cheese, pickles, onions, sauce and a small amount of seasoning. The restaurant will only combine these items just before the customer orders them so the Big Macs are hot and fresh when served.
- Finished products are goods that are ready for immediate sale to a customer. At any time, a restaurant will have a range of products ready for sale. Many of these will include finished products like Filet-o-Fish, Big Macs and side salads.

Ongoing communication between the central Restaurant Supply Planning team and individual restaurants helps manage the stock-effectively. A mixture of specialist stock controllers and employees who previously worked in the restaurants makes up the central team. This team of 14 regional planners works with around 80 restaurants each and communicates on a regular basis with them via email/telephone. Anything that would affect the number of customers visiting their restaurant needs to be logged with the team. This is taken into account in the calculating of the forecasts.

Supply planners work with the new stock control system, Manugistics, to ensure enough raw materials, e.g. beef, tomatoes, lettuce, leave the McDonald's distribution centres, such as Basingstoke. Forecasts are calculated using:

- Store-specific historic product mix data from the last two years.
- Store-specific and national causal factors. These specify dates for events such as national promotions and school holidays.
- Information from store managers about factors that might affect demand, e.g. road closures or local events and promotions.

Manugistics uses two years' worth of product mix history to produce forecasts for each restaurant. This uses time series analysis. The planner will apply a causal factor to the time series for the start and end date of this promotion. Using complex calculations, the graph then produces a forecast. Therefore, McDonald's restaurant managers need to ensure that the data they enter into the system is as accurate as possible. For example, each day restaurant managers record opening and closing stocks of key food items. They record all other items weekly. The store computer system identifies any stock count deviations from the last stock count so managers can investigate. Restaurants hold small buffer stock. This is an extra quantity of stock held to meet unexpected higher demand. It is also the point at which more goods are ordered—the re-order level.

Because McDonald's has taken much of the hard work out of stock management, restaurant managers are able to spend more time focusing on delivering McDonald's high standards of quality, service and cleanliness. Customers are happy because they can be sure the item they want is on the menu that day.

Discussion:

1. What is the role of restaurant managers at McDonald's in relation to stock control activities?

2. Why is the stock management system likely to improve over time?

3. What additional information might help central stock managers produce even more accurate figures?

Chapter 8

Transportation
运输

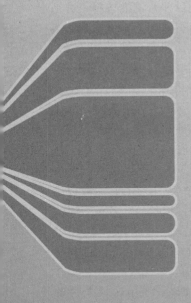

Alberta Coalmines
阿尔伯塔煤矿

Canada's largest **coalmines** are in the western province of Alberta. Unfortunately, most of the demand for coal comes from power stations in the population centre of southern **Ontario** over 3000 km away. The main competitors for coal in power stations are oil, gas, nuclear power and **hydroelectricity**. Coal is currently a popular choice as oil and gas are expensive, nuclear power has questions of long-team safety, and there is limited capacity for hydroelectricity. Alberta coal also has low **sulphur content**, which reduces the need for expensive exhaust gas **emission control** equipment. There are, however, obvious problems with transport. About three million tonnes of coal is shipped each year from Alberta to Ontario, with transport costs around $45 a **tonne**. The coal industry looks for ways of reducing this, and the alternatives considered are summarized below.

Rail and ship: this is the current practice, with coal transported by rail from the mine to a terminal on the Great Lakes (usually **Thunder Bay**) and then by ship to a lake side power station.

coalmine ['kəulmaɪn]
n. 煤矿

Ontario [ɒn'tɛərɪəu]
n. 安大略省；安大略湖

hydroelectricity ['haɪdrəʊɪlek'trɪsətɪ]
n. 水力电气

sulphur content [化学] 硫含量

emission control 排放控制；废气排出控制

tonne [tʌn]
n. [计量] 公吨（1000千克等于metric ton）

Thunder Bay 桑德贝(加拿大南部港市)

加拿大最大的煤矿是在西部省份阿尔伯塔省。遗憾的是大部分对煤炭的需求来自3000多千米以外，坐落在安大略省南部入口中心的发电厂。在发电厂，煤的主要竞争对手是石油、天然气、核能和水力发电。煤是目前普遍的选择，这是因为石油和天然气昂贵，核能的长期安全性受到质疑，并且水力发电能力有限。阿尔伯塔煤矿的硫含量比较低，降低了对昂贵的烟气排放设备的需求。然而，其中存在着明显的运输问题。每年约300万吨煤从阿尔伯塔运送到安大略省，运输费用大约为每吨45美元。煤炭行业正在寻找减少运输费用的途径，可考虑的选择总结如下。

铁路和船舶：这是目前的做法，铁路将煤炭从煤矿运输到终端大湖地区(通常是桑德贝)，然后用船运到湖边电站。

Direct rail shipment: moving coal by rail directly from the mine to a stockpile at a power station. This avoids the transfer to a ship, but replaces a sea journey with a considerably longer rail journey.

High efficiency rail: using newly designed rail cars that increase to maximum loads and reduce unit costs. With appropriate investment, high-efficiency trains can be used to replace conventional trains in either of the first two options.

West coast ports and Panama Canal: this carries coal by train to a west coast port such as **Vancouver**, transfers it to ship for the journey through the Panama Canal and back through the **St. Lawrence Seaway** to power stations in Ontario.

Coal/oil **agglomeration eastbound**: Alberta is a major oil producer and the transport of oil and coal can be combined. This crushes the coal at the mine and mixes it with crude oil to be pumped through a pipeline either directly to the power stations, or to a port on the Great Lakes. At the destination the **slurry** is separated, with coal being sent to the power stations and oil to markets in eastern Canada and the USA.

Energy bus, which avoids the movement of coal by generating electricity near to the mines and using an **interprovincial** electricity grid to send it for distribution in Ontario.

Analysing all the costs showed that a

Vancouver [væn'kuːvə]
n. 温哥华(加拿大主要港市)

St. Lawrence Seaway
圣劳伦斯河海道(美加两国合修的河道系统)

agglomeration [əˌɡlɒməˈreɪʃən]
n. 凝聚；结块

eastbound ['iːstbaund]
adj. 往东的；向东旅行的

slurry ['slɜːrɪ, 'slʌ-]
n. 泥浆；悬浮液

high-efficiency rail service from the mine to Thunder Bay, followed by ship to the power station gives the lowest cost. This is marginally cheaper than the current arrangement; but needs more capital investment.

interprovincial [ˌɪntəprə'vɪnʃəl] *adj*. 省际的；省与省之间的

运输。

分析所有的费用表明，最便宜的运输方式是：首先用高效铁路将煤炭从矿井运输至桑德贝，然后用船运至发电站。这比我们目前的运输方式便宜，但需要更多的资本投资。

Learning Objectives 【学习目标】

- To understand the definition of transportation.
- To learn the transport functionality and principles.
- To learn intermodal transportation.
- To learn letters for shipment.

Key Terms 【关键词】

freight transportation	货物运输	time and place utility	时间和空间效用
economy of distance	距离经济	economy of scale	规模经济
piggyback	驮背式运输	containership	集装箱船舶运输

Part 1　Definition of Transportation　运输的定义

Transportation is the creation of time and place utility. When goods are moved to places where they have higher value than they had at the places from which they **originated**, they have place utility. Time utility means that this service occurs when it is needed. Under the condition of meeting the time requirements of customers, the utility of time and space is to realize the spatial transfer of goods from the place of supply to the place of demand.

originate [ə'rɪdʒəneɪt] *vi*. 发源；产生

运输是时间和空间效用的产物。当货物转移到比在原产地具有更高价值的地方时，它们就发挥了空间效用。时间效用意味着服务在其需要时及时提供。时间和空间效用是在满足客户时间要求的情况下，实现货物从供应地到需求地的空间转移。

Transportation should not be viewed as the simple movement of persons or things through space. The user is actually purchasing a bundle of services from a carrier at a certain cost. The bundle of services includes choosing carriers and modes of transportation, with different prices frequently in effect from the different services. If the user focuses on the **simplistic** version of transportation, that is, movement through space, the lowest-priced service will be selected. However, the higher-priced carrier might the best choice because of **superior** service, which will result in lower costs in other areas, such as inventory.

Transportation is also one of the economic factors in the production of goods and services. The basic function of Transportation is to provide the market with access to the resultant products. Transportation plays a major role in the spatial relations of **geographic** points, and it also affects temporal relationships. Transportation demand is essentially a request to move a given amount of cargo or people within a specific distance. Therefore, the demand unit for transportation is measured in weight×distance or passenger×distance. For freight, the demand unit is the ton×mile and for people it is the passenger×mile.

The ton×mile is not a **homogenous** unit. The demand for 200 ton×miles of

simplistic
[sɪm'plɪstɪk]
adj. 过分简单化的

superior
[sju:'pɪrɪə, sju:pə-]
adj. 上级的；优秀的，出众的

geographic
[dʒɪə'græfɪk]
adj. 地理的；地理学的

homogenous
[hɒ'mɒdʒənəs]
adj. [生物] 同质的；同类的

运输不能被看作是人或物在空间上的简单移动的过程。客户实际上是以一定的资金向承运商购买一系列的服务。这一系列的服务包括选择不同的承运商和不同的运输方式，实际上通常是从事不同价格的不同服务。如果客户只需要简单的运输方式，即只要实现货物的空间移动，那么可以选择低价的服务。然而，较高价格的托运有可能成为最佳的选择，这是因为高质量的服务在库存等其他方面能降低成本。

运输也是在商品生产和服务过程的一种经济活动。运输的基本功能是向市场提供最终产品的通道。运输在连接地理空间之间起着重大作用，它也对时间的调整产生影响。运输实际是将一定数量的货物或人进行一定距离的移动过程。因此，运输是以货物的重量×距离或乘客数量×距离为单位来衡量的。对于货运而言，衡量单位是吨×英里，而对乘客而言，则是乘客数量×英里。

吨×英里不是一个同性质的单位。200吨×英里的货物运输需求，可以表示200吨货物移动了1英里，

freight transportation could be for moving 200 tons one mile, 100 tons two miles, one ton 200 miles, or any other combination of weight and distance that equals 200 ton×miles. In addition, the unique transportation requirements for direction, equipment, and service will vary among customers with a 200 ton×mile demand. For example, the demand for 200 ton×miles of ice cream from Pittsburgh might require movement in all directions and a refrigerated vehicle with same-day delivery, whereas the demand for 200 ton×miles of **gasoline** from **Philadelphia** might be movement to north, south, and west in a tank vehicle with next-day delivery.

The above examples are aimed at **delineating** the heterogeneous nature of the transportation demand unit. The same demand unit might have a different cost of producing and different user service requirements. However, no other measurement unit reflects the basic weight and distance components of freight transportation demand.

gasoline
[ˈgæsəliːn]
n. 汽油

Philadelphia
[ˌfɪləˈdelfjə; -fɪə]
n. 费城(美国宾夕法尼亚州东南部港市)

delineate
[dɪˈlɪnɪeɪt]
vt. 描绘；描写

或者100吨货物移动了2英里，也可以是1吨货物移动了200英里，或是任何等于200吨×英里的其他重量和距离的组合。此外，因为各种运输方向、设备和服务方式不同，200吨×英里中，货物重量和运输距离的组合也不同。例如，如果从匹兹堡出发，采用冷藏车向任何方向进行200吨×英里的冰激凌运输时，只需一天内就可完成；而从费城往北、南和西方向，用油轮运输200吨×英里的汽油时，需要两天完成任务。

上述的例子旨在描述运输需求量的复合特征(由不同部分组成)。同一单位的数值可能有不同的生产成本和不同的客户服务需求。然而，没有其他计量单位可以同时反映需求货运的基本重量和距离的组成。

Part 2　Transport Functionality and Principles 运输的作用和原则

1.Transport Functionality

Transportation enterprises provide two major services: product movement and product storage.

● Product movement

Whether in the form of materials, components, **work-in-process**, or finished goods, the basic value provided by transportation is to move inventory to the next stage of the business process. The primary transportation value is product movement up and down the supply chain. The performance of transportation is **vital** to procurement, manufacturing, and market distribution. Transportation also plays a key role in the performance of reverse logistics. Without **reliable** transportation, most commercial activities could not function. Transportation consumes many resources, such as time, financial, and environmental resources.

● Product storage

A less visible aspect of transportation is product storage. While a product is in a transportation vehicle, it is being stored. There fore, transportation vehicles can also be used for product storage at shipment origin or **destination**, but they are comparatively expensive storage facilities. Since the primary

work-in-process
n. 半成品

vital ['vaɪtl]
adj. 对关系重大

reliable [rɪ'laɪəbl]
adj. 可靠的；可信赖的

destination [ˌdestɪ'neɪʃən]
n. 目的地，终点

1. 运输的作用

运输企业主要提供了两种类型的服务：产品移动和产品存储。

● 产品移动

无论运输的对象是原材料、部件、在制品还是产成品，运输服务的基本价值就在于将库存货物运送到业务流程中下一个确定的地点。运输的主要价值是使产品在供应链中进行移动。对于采购、生产和市场分销而言，运输渠道是否通畅将起到至关重要的作用。运输对于逆向物流的重要性也同样不可忽视。如果没有可靠的运输作为保障，很多商业活动都无法正常地开展下去。运输过程中消耗了多种资源，如时间资源、财力资源和环境资源等。

● 产品存储

运输所提供的另一种服务就是产品的存储，但是这种服务不太被人关注。产品被装载在运输工具上的时候，实际上就等同于被储存起来了。因此，运输工具在运货的起点或终点也可以起到储存产品的作用，但是相

value of transportation is movement; a vehicle committed to storage is not otherwise available for transport. A trade-off exists between using a transportation vehicle and temporarily placing products in a warehouse. If the inventory involved is **scheduled** to move within a few days to a different location, the cost of unloading, warehousing, and reloading the product may exceed the temporary charge of using the transportation vehicle for storage.

Another transport service having storage implications is diversion. Diversion occurs when a shipment destination is changed after a product is in transit. For example, the destination of a product initially shipped from Chicago to Los Angeles may be changed to Seattle while in transit. Formerly, the telephone was used to implement **diversion** strategies. Today, satellite communication among shippers, carriers' headquarters, and vehicles facilitates more efficient diversion. While diversion is primarily used to improve logistical responsiveness, it also impacts the duration of in-transit storage.

So although costly, product storage in transportation vehicles may be justified from a total cost or performance perspective when loading or unloading costs, capacity **constraints**, and ability

schedule
['ʃedju:l, -dʒu:l]
vt. 安排，计划；将列入计划表

diversion
[daɪ'vɜ:ʃən]
n. 转移

constraint
[kən'streɪnt]
n. [数] 约束；强制

对而言，它们是较为昂贵的储存设备。运输的主要价值在于实现货物的移动，而利用运输工具来进行储存就无法达到运送产品的目的，也就实现不了运输的价值。究竟是应该使用运输工具进行存储，还是应该暂时将产品存放在仓库中，需要人们对这两种方式的优缺点进行分析，做出权衡。如果产品要在几天之内运送到一个新的地点，那么卸货、储存、再装货的费用就可能会超过暂时使用运输工具进行储存的费用。

转移是另一种运输服务，它也具有临时储存产品的功能。当运货地点发生改变而产品仍处在运输途中时，我们就可以使用转移的方法。举例来说，产品起初是由芝加哥运至洛杉矶，然而在运输途中，产品的目的地改为西雅图(在这种情况下，就需要转移这项运输服务)。以前，人们通常使用电话来实现转移；而现在，托运人、承运商总部、运输车辆之间则通过卫星通信技术来进行交流，实现了更加高效的货物转移。转移主要是为了提高物流的响应速度，但它同时也会对在途库存有所影响。

to extend lead time are taken into consideration.

2. Transport Principles

There are two **fundamental** economic principles that impact transportation efficiency: economy of scale and economy of distance.

- Economy of scale

Economy of scale in transportation is the cost per unit of weight decreases as the size of a shipment increases. For example, **truckload** shipments utilizing an entire trailer's capacity have lower cost per pound than smaller shipments that utilize a limited portion of vehicle capacity. It is also generally true that larger-capacity transportation vehicles such as trains and vessels are less costly per unit of weight than smaller-capacity vehicles such as trucks and airplanes. Transportation economies of scale exist because fixed cost associated with transporting a load is allocated over the increased weight. Fixed costs include administration related to scheduling, cost of equipment, parking fee to position vehicles for loading or unloading, and invoicing. Such costs are considered fixed because they do not vary with shipment size. In other words, it costs as much to administer a 100-pound shipment as one weighing 1000 pounds.

- Economy of distance

Economy of distance refers to

fundamental [ˌfʌndəˈmentəl]
adj. 基本的，根本的

truckload [ˈtrʌkləud]
n. 一货车的容量；货车荷载

因此，尽管使用运输车辆来储存产品的成本很高，但是如果考虑装卸费用、存储容量约束、延长提前期等因素的影响，从总成本和运作绩效的角度来看，这种方法也具有一定的可行性。

2．运输的原则

规模经济和距离经济这两个基本的经济原则对运输的效率有显著的影响。

- 规模经济

在运输中，规模经济是指，当运输产品的规模增加时，每单位重量的成本就会降低。例如，与只利用运输车辆一部分容量的小型运输方式(如零担运输)相比，完全利用车辆全部容积的大型运输(如整车运输)的单位重量的运输成本要低得多。同理，大型运输工具，如火车或轮船，单位重量的运输成本要远远低于卡车或飞机等小型运输工具。之所以在运输领域中存在规模经济，是因为增加运输的重量之后，固定成本会得到进一步的分摊。运输的固定成本包括与安排有关的管理费用、设备费用、装卸货时的停车费以及发票费用等。这些费用不随着运输规模的变化而变化，因此它们属于固定成本。换句话

decreased transportation cost per unit of weight as distance increases. For example, a shipment of 800 miles will cost less to perform than two shipments of the same weight each moving 400 miles. Transportation economy of distance is often referred to as the **tapering** principle. The rationale for distance economies is similar to that of economies of scale. Specifically, longer distance allow fixed cost to be spread over more miles, resulting in lower per mile charges.

These principles are important when evaluating transportation alternatives. The goal from a transportation perspective is to maximize the size of the load and the distance being shipped while still meeting customer service expectations.

tapering
['teɪpərɪŋ]
adj. 尖端细的；锥状的

说，也就是运输 100 磅产品的固定成本与运输 1000 磅产品的固定成本是相同的。

- 距离经济

距离经济是指每单位重量的运输费用随着距离的增加而减少。例如，将产品运输 800 英里所需要的费用，比将同样重量的产品分两次运送 400 英里的费用要低。运输中的距离经济也常常被称为远距离递减原则。距离经济的原理与规模经济基本相似。具体来说，距离的增加使固定成本在更大的基数上进行了分摊，因此降低了单位距离的成本。

对不同的运输方式进行评估时，企业必须对规模经济和距离经济的影响加以考虑。因此，从运输的角度来看，实现运输产品的数量和运输距离的最大化，同时充分满足客户要求，就是运输任务的主要目标。

Part 3　Intermodal Transportation 多式联运

Intermodal transportation combines two or more modes to take advantage of the inherent economics of each and thus provides an integrated service at lower total cost. Many efforts have been made over the years to integrate

多式联运将两种或两种以上的运输方式结合在一起，它利用每种运输方式的优势，以较低的总成本提供了一种综合性的运输服务。多年来，为了将不同的运输方式结合起来，人们付出

different transportation modes. Initial attempts at inter modal coordination **traced back to** the early 1920s, but during that early period, cooperation was restrained by restrictions designed to limit monopoly practices. Intermodal offerings began to develop more successfully during the 1950s with the **advent** of integrated rail and motor service commonly termed piggyback service. This common intermodal arrangement combines the flexibility of motor for short distance with the low **line-haul** cost associated with rail for longer distance. The popularity of such offerings has increased significantly as a means to achieve more efficient and effective transportation.

Technically, coordinated or intermodal transportation could be arranged among all basic modes. Descriptive **jargon** such as piggyback, fishyback, trainship, and airtruck has become standard transportation terms.

1. Piggyback/TOFC/COFC

The best known and most widely used intermodal system is the trailer (TOFC) or container (COFC) on a flatcar. Containers are the boxes utilized for intermodal product storage and movement among motor freight, railroads, and water transportation. Containers are typically 8 feet wide, 8

trace back to
追溯到

advent
['ædvənt]
n. 到来；出现

line-haul
['laɪnˌhɔːl]
n. 长途运输

jargon
['dʒɑːg(ə)n]
n. 行话，术语

了大量努力。实现多种运输方式的协调发展可以追溯到 20 世纪 20 年代初期，然而，当时政府为了防止出现垄断而制定的限制因素抑制了运输方式之间的协作。随着铁路和汽车运输联合运输服务的出现，多种模式运输在 20 世纪 50 年代开始有了较快的发展。当时，这种综合性服务被称为"驮背式服务"。这种联运方式将汽车在短途运输上的灵活性与火车在长距离运输中长途运输成本较低的特点有机地结合在一起，形成了一种更加经济有效的运输手段。因此，这种多式联运的方式很快就风靡一时。

从技术的角度来讲，协调式的货运或多式联运的运输完全可以在基本运输方式的基础上实现。那些具有描述性质的专业术语，如驮背式运输、背负式运输、火车渡运以及运货飞机承载等，已经成为标准的运输专用词汇。

1. 驮背式运输/拖车运输/集装箱运输

运输行业中最广为人知的多式联运方式是在轻型运货车上使用的拖车运输(TOFC)和集装箱运输(COFC)。集装箱是一种货箱，通常用来储存联运的货物，以及在汽车运输、铁路运输、水路运输中完成货物的装卸。最

feet high, 20 or 40 feet long, and do not have highway wheels. **Trailers** and containers are of similar width and height but trailers can be as long as 53 feet and have highway wheels. As the name implies, a trailer or a container is placed on a railroad **flatcar** for some portion of the intercity line-haul and pulled by a truck at origin and destination. Line-haul cost is the expense to move railcars or trucks among cities. With the original development of TOFC, various combinations of trailers or containers with flatcars — double stacks, for instance — have increased significantly.

While the TOFC concept facilitates direct transfer between rail and motor carriage, it also has several technical limitations. The placement of a trailer with highway wheels attached, transferred to a **railcar**, can lead to wind resistance, damage, and weight problems. The use of containers reduces these potential problems, as they can be double **stacked** and are easily transferred to water carriers. However, they require special equipment for over-the-road delivery or pickup.

2. Containership

Fishyback, trainship, and containerships are examples of the oldest forms of intermodal transport. They

trailer
['treɪlə]
n. 拖车

flatcar
['flætkɑː]
n. 无盖货车；平台型铁路货车

railcar ['reɪlkɑː]
n. 气动车，轨道车

stack [stæk]
vi. 堆积，堆叠

常见的集装箱一般是 8 英尺宽、8 英尺高、20 英尺或 40 英尺长，集装箱的底部没有车轮。拖车虽然与集装箱的高度和宽度差不多，但是它的长度却可以达到 53 英尺，并且底部装有车轮，能够在公路上行驶。拖车和集装箱都可以放在铁路平板货车上，用以完成城际间的部分长途运输。此外，在始发站和终点站，拖车和集装箱都是由卡车来进行牵引运输的。长途运输的成本就是在城市之间完成有轨机车或卡车运输的费用。随着 TOFC 的出现，各种将拖车或集装箱与铁路平板货车相结合的产物都得到了极大发展，例如双层列车。

尽管 TOFC 的出现有利于在铁路运输与公路运输之间直接实现货物的转移，但是 TOFC 也存在一定程度的技术局限性。将装有车轮的拖车放置到有轨机车上，可能会导致阻碍通风、损坏或者超重等问题。而集装箱的使用则减少了这些潜在问题，因为它们可以被双层堆放，而且转到水路运输很方便。但是，需要注意的一点是，利用集装箱进行收货和送货时需要使用专用设备。

2. 集装箱船舶运输

背负式运输、火车渡运、集装箱船舶运输都是一些比较传统的多式联运形式。它们都需要借

utilize waterways, which are one of the least expensive modes for line-haul movement.

A variant of this intermodal option is the land bridge concept that moves containers in a combination of sea and rail transport. The land bridge is commonly used for containers moving between Europe and the Pacific Rim to reduce the time and expense of all-water transport. For example, containers are shipped to the West Coast of North America from the Pacific Rim, loaded onto railcars for movement to the East Coast, and then reloaded onto ships for movement to Europe. The land bridge concept is based on the benefit of ocean and rail combinations that utilize a single **tariff**, which is lower than the combined total cost of two separate rates.

3. Coordinated Air-Truck

Another form of intermodal transport combines air and truck. Local cartage is a vital part of every air movement because air freight must eventually move from the airport to the final delivery destination. Air-truck movements usually provide service and flexibility comparable to straight motor freight.

Air-truck is commonly used to provide **premium** package services, such as those offered by UPS and

tariff ['tærɪf]
n. 关税表；收费表

premium ['pri:mɪəm]
n. 保险费，额外费用；奖金

助于水路运输，对于长途运输来讲，水运是最便宜的运输方式。

多式联运方式衍生出一种新的概念——大陆桥。大陆桥是指将铁路与海路运输相结合，共同运输集装箱货物。大陆桥在欧洲与环太平洋地区的集装箱运输业务中得到了广泛的应用，它既可以节约时间，又可以减少水路运输的总费用。举例来说，先将集装箱从环太平洋沿岸运送到北美的西海岸，再将集装箱放置在火车上送到美国的东海岸，然后通过水路运输将其运到欧洲。考虑到将水运与铁路运输结合后能够降低运输成本，产生可观收益的同时，使用这种方式只用上缴一份关税，比独立上缴海路与铁路两部分的关税总额要低，所以才产生了大陆桥的概念。

3.空运和陆运之间的协调

另一种多式联运方式是空运和陆运的结合。本地的货车运输是空运的一个重要组成部分，因为必须使用货车把空运的货物运送到最终目的地。空运－陆运的联运方式通常提供的服务和具有的灵活性，可以与直接的汽车运输相媲美。

空运－陆运的联运方式通常适用于需要额外付费的加急运输服务，如UPS和DHL所提

DHL, but can also be used for more standard freight applications for several reasons. First, there is a lack of air freight service to smaller cities in the United States. Smaller cities are often served by narrow-body aircraft and commuter planes that are not equipped to handle freight. Thus, motor carriage into small cities from **metropolitan** airports provides a needed service at a competitive cost. Second, package carriers, while suited to serve small cities, have limited ability to handle heavy freight. Package carriers that are focused on smaller parcels and materials handling systems are limited in ability to handle heavy freight. As a result, many air carriers have extended their motor freight range to provide service to expanded geographical areas.

The concept of intermodalism appeals to both shippers and carriers due to the economic leverage of linking two modes. In fact, many authorities believe the only way to maintain a strong national transportation network is to encourage and foster intermodalism. Efforts to increase intermodalism are of prime interest to logistical planners because such development expands options available in logistical system design.

metropolitan
[metrə'pɒlɪt(ə)n]
adj. 大都市的

供的服务。同时，这种联运方式还可以用于一些标准货物的运输，其原因如下。第一，在美国，空运的辐射范围并没有遍布到小型城市，因此小型城市的航空服务通常是由一些小型货机或者在短途间进行往返的飞机来完成的，这些飞机不具备运输大量货物的能力。这样，在大城市的飞机场与小城市之间使用汽车运输就成了必然，同时，这种服务的成本还颇具竞争力。第二，为小城市提供包裹配送服务的运输公司基本上不具备处理大型货物的能力。那些以小包裹和其他货物为主要服务对象的运输公司，往往由于自身能力的限制，不能运送大型货物。于是，许多空运运输公司就拓展了自身汽车运输的范围，以便能够在更大区域内提供服务。

多式联运的方式之所以对托运人和承运人都具有很强的吸引力，是因为它将两种或两种以上运输方式结合起来，发挥了经济杠杆作用。事实上，许多政府都认为，要维持一个强有力的国家运输系统，唯一的方法就是鼓励并且促进联合运输的蓬勃发展。物流管理者最感兴趣的是如何加快多式联运的发展，因为随着联合运输的发展，企业在进行物流系统设计时就具有更大的选择权。

Chapter 8 Transportation
运输

Part 4 Specimen Letters 信函范例

1. Request for Advance Shipment

May 26, 2019

Dear Mr. Han,

Request for Advance Shipment(Order No.12402)

With reference to the above order, we would like to ask for changing the scheduled date of delivery from June 15 to June 1, due to market demand.

We realize that the change of delivery date may cause your inconvenience. Please try to arrange the shipment as early as possible if the suggested delivery date cannot be met.

We apologize for any inconvenience caused by early shipment, and look forward to your reply to our request soon.

Yours sincerely,

Tianming Liu(Ms.)
Manager

1. 要求提早装运

韩先生：

要求提早装运(订单编号：12402)

就以上订单的货品交货日期原为 6 月 15 日，现因市场需要，欲提前于 6 月 1 日交货。

若非急切需要，本公司亦不敢提出此项要求。如货品未能在以上提议日期交货，亦请贵公司把交货日期尽量提前。

对于提早装运该批货品而引起贵公司的不便，本公司深感歉意，敬悉谅解。请早日回复确认。

经理
刘天明
2019 年 5 月 26 日

2. Proposal for Partial Shipment

May 27, 2019
Dear Ms. Liu,

Proposal for Partial Shipment(Order No.12402)

Thank you for your letter of May 26 requesting for advance shipment of goods for the above order.

We have tried to arrange an advance shipment for your order but regret to inform you that we are not able to comply with your full request. The best we can help is to arrange an advance shipment for 500 wineglasses on June 1. The remaining 500 wineglasses will be dispatched on June 15, as agreed on the contract.

We have tried our best to make the arrangement. If you agree to the above proposal for partial shipment, please amend the relevant L/C and fax us the amended copy. We look forward to your prompt reply and will ask the manufacturer to make advance delivery accordingly.

Yours sincerely,

Qiang Han(Mr.)
Manager

2. 提议分批装运

刘小姐：

提议分批装运(订单编号：12402)

收到贵公司 5 月 26 日的来函，要求提早装运以上订单的货品。

本公司深知贵公司装运的急切性，已尽量做出安排，唯恐未能完全达到贵公司的要求。现提议先于 6 月 1 日装运 500 件玻璃酒杯，剩余的 500 件则按合同列明，于 6 月 15 日装运。

本公司已尽量根据贵公司要求做出安排。如贵公司同意以上装运建议，请修改有关信用证，准许分批装运，并传真本公司确认。请早日回复，以便通知厂商提前交货。

经理

韩强

2019 年 5 月 27 日

Summary 本章小结

This chapter introduces the definition of transportation. The transport functionality and principles are described. The importance of logistics channels in international transportation is discussed. At last, letters for shipment are introduced.

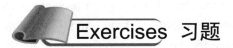

Exercises 习题

Questions for Review 复习题

1. What is the definition of transportation?
2. What is the transport functionality?
3. What are the transport principles?
4. What are the major types of international air freight operations?
5. What are the major logistics channels in international transportation?

True or False 判断对错

1. There is a kind of measurement unit reflecting the basic weight and distance components of freight transportation demand.
2. Economy of distance refers to increased transportation cost per unit of weight as distance increases.
3. The widespread use of seaborne containers has brought about hopes of standardizing land vehicles for carrying containers on the land.
4. Transportation is usually the biggest logistic costs for most companies.
5. Container logistics management is becoming a core strategy for large shipping companies for its fast loading and unloading process, safe transportation and goods storage.

Topic for Discussion 讨论话题

Each product has its special characteristics and requirement for transportation service, so for each type of product, there is only one transport mode that can provide the best service, do you agree?

Logistic English dialogue 物流英语对话

Talk About the Mode of Transportation

A: Good morning, I really meet some trouble about how to transport my goods to America. Would you give me some suggestion?

B: Don't be nervous. There are several modes of transportation to ship your goods to America. And many logistics companies are in this line. You can first take account for the modes of transportation, and then try to find a good transport company or a freight forwarder.

A: Certainly. We're thinking about this. But the main problem is that we ask for a prompt shipment in early August. But today is 20th of June. And I was informed by our shipping department yesterday that liner space for America up to the end of the next month has been fully booked up.

B: That's quite urgent. But tramps are still available.

A: Yes, but tramps are after all scarce. And I'm not sure whether there is enough remained cargo space to be obtained.

B: Have you thought of connecting steamer? So far as I know, the HKMW Co. has an extra liner sailing from Hong Kong to America around the mid of July. If you could manage to catch that ship, everything will be all right.

A: Really? It sounds great. I'll contact them immediately. Thanks a lot!

Case Study 案例分析题

Logistic Blossoms in Holland

Nothing is more Dutch than the 11-million-square-foot Aalsmeer Flower Auction, which is the world's largest flower marketplace. Each morning starting at 5:30 a.m., 5400 growers sell 20 million flowers to 1050 buyers in a carefully orchestrated auction process. Millions of flowers and plants arrive from all over the world in the late afternoon and evening, and by late the next morning they are all gone and on their way by truck, air and even ocean container to customers in Europe, Asia and North America.

Aalsmeer is near Schiphol, so 95 percent of the foreign flowers come through the airport and many of the products also leave the same way. There is a shift to ocean. The auction is about 12 kilometers from Schiphol Airport, but the congestion makes this short trip take 30 to 40 minutes. A direct underground connection was considered but was too expensive. The competition is Flora Holland.

"We are in the logistics business," says CEO Timo Huges, who spent most of his career with 3PL Frans Maas. "It just so happens that our products are flowers."

Huges, in fact, sees the future of the flower auction more as a 4PL helping buyers and sellers manage their logistics function rather than merely serving as a marketplace.

The buyers are essentially in logistics as well. Paul Holex buys flowers at the Aalsmeer Auction and ships them to wholesalers in North America and Japan. One third of his business is to the U.S. rather than Schiphol. He ships via American Airlines out of the U.K., so he builds pallets of 210000 stems that are containerized at Heathrow for shipment to customers in the U.S. The existing air capacity and price is limited and expensive, so he is beginning to ship via ocean container. Plants are put in stasis by lowering the temperature to just above freezing and placed in the containers at his facility adjacent to the auction site. He will move 30 containers next year to see how this system works.

"There is far less handling of the stems and better temperature control with ocean containers," he says. "Air freight may be faster, but too much handling and poor cooling facilities in the U.S. can damage the flowers."

With a net margin of about 1.4 percent shipped by air, lower shipping costs and reducing damage can make a big profit difference.

Turnover in 2004 was 1.63 billion euros. Its massive complex (1 million square meters) has a 13-kilometre state-of-the-art internal transport system, the Aalsmeer Shuttle, conveying floricultural products on an electronically controlled aerial rail system from auctions at the distribution centre across the motorway to customers in the south, a recently developed business park that is home to some 25 wholesalers and exporters.

Discussion: What are the strong and weak points of each transportation mode mentioned?

Chapter 9

Logistics Documents
物流单证

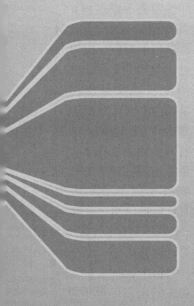

Electronic Delivery of Documents
单据的电子支付

In the modern world, the document software can be used to create, view, e-mail, and print the formatted document. Lots of logistics documents can be printed. For example, an easy-to-use online **bill** of lading generator will save time and provide the documents instantly.

The electronic delivery of the bill of lading can speed up the trade finance process. It can reduce the cycle time for forwarding and presentation of documents. The exporter gets paid more quickly and the importer gets title to the goods sooner. It also **eliminates** the risk of errors and reduces the costs related to manual document preparation.

Logistics documents are **indispensable** in the logistics services, which mainly include letter of credit, bill of lading, multimodal transport documents, **invoice**, insurance policy, inspection certificate, certificate of origin, packing list, air waybill, and shipper's export declaration, etc.

bill [bɪl]
n. [金融] 票据；钞票；清单

eliminate [ɪ'lɪmɪneɪt]
vt. 消除；排除

indispensable [ˌɪndɪs'pensəbl]
adj. 不可缺少的；绝对必要的

invoice ['ɪnvɔɪs]
n. 发票

在现代社会，单据软件能够用来创建、浏览、电邮和打印有格式的单据。许多物流单据都能打印。例如，一个方便使用的在线海运提单生成器能够节约时间，立即提供单据。

海运提单的电子提交可以加快贸易融资过程。它能够减少代理的循环周期和出示单据的时间。出口方可以更快地得到支付，进口方可以更快地取得货物的所有权。它还可以减小手工制作单据可能出现错误的风险和减少相应的成本。

企业在提供物流服务中，物流单据是必不可少的，主要包括信用证、海运提单、多式联运单据、发票、保险单、检验证书、原产地证书、装箱单、航空货运单和托运人的出口申报单等。

 Learning Objectives【学习目标】

- To understand the definition of logistics documents.
- To learn how to draw up or write main logistics documents.

Chapter 9 Logistics Documents
物流单证

- To know about letter of credit.

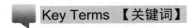Key Terms 【关键词】

logistics documents	物流单据	air waybill	(航)空运单
bill of lading	提(货)单	commercial invoice	商业发票
packing list	装箱单	certificate of origin	原产地证明(书)

Part 1 Documents in Logistics 物流单据

1. Bill of Lading

A bill of lading (B/L) is used for sea shipment and is a certificate of ownership of goods. It must be presented at the port of final destination by the importer in order to claim goods. As a document of title, the bill of lading is also a **negotiable** document and you may sell the goods by **endorsing** or handing the bill of lading over to another authorized party, even while the goods are still at sea. Although negotiable bills of lading are commonly used, in some countries, they are still unacceptable. You have to be sure that a negotiable B/L is accepted in your country. Otherwise, a non-negotiable B/L is issued.

The B/L is a formal, signed receipt for a specified number of packed cargos, which is given to the export agent by the carrier when it receives the **consignment**. If the cargo is in apparently good condition and properly packed when the carrier receives them, the bill of lading, is marked

negotiable
[nɪ'ɡəʊʃɪəbl]
adj. 可通过谈判解决的；可协商的

endorse [ɪn'dɔːs]
vt. 背书；签署；在背面签名

consignment
[kən'saɪnmənt]
n. 委托；运送；托付物

1. 提单

提单是海洋运输中货物所有权的证明，是进口商为在目的港领取货物时提交的单据。作为物权凭证，提单也是一种可议付的文件，即便货物还在海运途中，也可以通过背书将货物出售或者转给其他被授权方。虽然可议付式提单比较普遍，但是仍有些国家禁止或限制它的使用。所以你必须确认这张可议付式提单在你的国家是可被接受的，否则，就应该开具不可议付式提单。

提单是为特定的批量包装物而签署的正式收据，当船运公司收到被托运的货物时，提单就由船运公司签发给出口代理商。如果货物交给船运公司时外观整齐、包装完好，此时提单就

as "clean". The carrier thus accepts full **liability** for the cargo described in the bill. Below is a sample B/L(See Figure 9-1).

liability
[ˌlaɪəˈbɪlətɪ]
n. 责任；债务

被称为"清洁"提单。这样船东将为提单所表述的货物负完全责任。提单样图如图 9-1 所示。

SHIPPER TIANJIN TEXTILE EXPORT CORP. NO.×××　ROAD,TIANJIN,CHINA TEL:86-020-629928××			B/L NO. <u>CANE100318</u>		
CONSIGNEE TO ORDER OF CITI BANK,NEW YORK NO.×××　ROAD, NEW YORK, U.S.A TEL:01-808825XX			**IN APPARENT GOOD ORDER ON BOARD B/L** ×××　OCEAN SHIPPING (GROUP) CO. ORINGINAL COMBINED TRANSPORT BILL OF LADING		
NOTIFY PARTY THE XYZ TRADING CO. NO.×××　ROAD, NEW YORK,U.S.A TEL:01-908825XX					
PLACE OF RECEIPT		PORT OF LOADING SHANGHAI			
PORT OF DISCHARGE NEW YORK		PLACE OF DELIVERY THE XYZ TRADING CO.			
OCEAN VESSEL JOHNSENT V.002		VOYAGE NO. 002			
MARKS N/M	NOS. & KINDS OF PKGS 1 PC A WOODEN BOX LINED WITH BATH FOAM	DESCRIPTION OF GOODS WELDING TESTING DEVICE 600×248×389CM FREIGHT PREPAID		G.W.(kg) 256KGS	MEAS(CBM) 57.88CBM
FREIGHT & CHARGES USD ××× DECLARED　VALUE CHARGE	IN WITNESS WHERE OF THE CARRIER OR HIS AGENT HAS SIGNED THE ABOVE STATED NUMBER OF BILL OF LADING ALL OF THIS TENOR AND DATE, ONE OF WHICH BEING ACCOMPLISHED THE OTHERS TO STAND VOID.				
TERMS AND CONDITIONS AS PER BACK HEREOF	PLACE OF ISSUE: SHANGHAI				
	DATE OF ISSUE: 2020-8-15				
	ON BOARD DATE 2020-8-20				
FREIGHT AND CHARGES FREIGHT PREPAID	SIGNED (FOR THE MASTER) BY: ×××　OCEAN SHIPPING (GROUP) CO.				
NO. OF ORIGINAL B(s)/L 3/3	SIGNED FOR THE CARRIER ×××　OCEAN SHIPPING(GROUP)CO.			SIGNATURE	

Figure 9-1　Bill of Lading

图 9-1　提单

From Figure 9-1, we can see that a bill of lading should contain information including name of the consignor, name of the consignee, name of the master of the vessel, name of the vessel, place of departure and destination, price of the freight, and the marks and numbers of the goods being shipped. There are usually three copies of one original B/L. One of them is commonly sent to the consignee on board with the goods; another is sent to the consignee by mail or via other channels; and the third one is kept by the merchant or shipper.

2. Air Waybill

An air waybill is used for air transport. It is an evidence of a transportation contract. This document for air freight is far simpler than that for ocean freight, such as B/L. It is:

- A receipt from the airline **acknowledging** that it has received the consignment from the shipper;
- A contract between the shipper and the airline for moving the goods;
- An instruction sheet;
- A customs declaration;
- A bill for the freight;
- A certificate of insurance, if the amount and extent of insurance are included in it.

The air waybill is an internationally **standardized** document, printed in English and in the language of the carrier. Unlike the bill of lading, the air waybill does not

acknowledge [əkˈnɒlɪdʒ] *vt.* 承认；告知已收到

standardized [ˈstændədaɪzd] *adj.* 标准的；标准化的

由图 9-1 可见，提单应该包含出货人姓名、收货人姓名、船东名称、船名、启运港及目的港名、运费，另需在空白处注明所运货物的唛头和数量。提单通常是一式三份正本。一份随船交给收货人，另一份通过邮件或其他渠道寄给收货人，而第三份则由出口商或托运人保留。

2. 空运单

空运单适用于航空运输，是(双方)为运输而签订的合约的书面证明。这种空运单据远比海运单据如提单要简单得多。它是：

- 航空公司确认已收到发货人货物的收货凭证；
- 托运人和航空公司关于货物运输的合约；
- 一份指示单；
- 海关报关单；
- 一份货运单；
- 一份保险单(如果保险的金额和范围在单据中被注明)。

空运单是一种国际标准化格式的单据，用英文和航空公司国家的母语印制。与提单不同的是，空运单并

represent the ownership of goods. The air waybill is not a negotiable document and the shipper does not lose ownership of the goods after handing it over to the airline. The exporter only has to present his copy of the air waybill to the airline to exercise his "right of **disposal**" to the goods. He can do this at any time and so can:

- Stop the goods at any point of their journey;
- Have the goods delivered to a different consignee mentioned in the air waybill;
- **Recall** the shipment.

The air waybill must be filled either by the shipper himself, the air cargo agent or the airline, and become a valid document when both the shipper and the airline representative have signed it.

There are three copies of one original air waybill (See Figure 9-2) for:

- The carrier (the airline). The airline uses copies for various purposes, such as **customs clearance**, as an invoice and so on.
- The **consignee** (receiver). A copy of air waybill is carried with the consignment and delivered to the customer at the airport of destination.
- The **consignor** (shipper). A copy of air waybill will be returned to him as a receipt and evidence of his freight contract with the airline.

disposal [dɪs'pəuzəl] *n.* 处理；支配

recall [rɪ'kɔːl, 'riːkɔːl] *vt.* 召回；取消

customs clearance [贸易] 海关放行；结关

consignee [ˌkɒnsaɪ'niː] *n.* 收件人；受托者

consignor [kən'saɪnə] *n.* 发货人；货主；委托者

不享有货物的所有权，它也不可议付。发货人虽将货物转交给承运人，但没有失去对货物的所有权。出口商仅需出示空运单复印件给航空公司，就可行使其对货物的支配权，他可随时：

- 中止在途的货物运输；
- 将货物转交给空运单上提及的另一个收货人；
- 召回货物。

空运单必须由发货人自己、空运代理人或航空公司填写，当发货人和承运人代表都签字之后即刻生效。

一份空运单为一式三联(如图9-2所示)，分别给：

- 承运人(航空公司)。承运人可用空运单副本做多种用途，比如可用于海关清关、发票等。
- 收货人(收件者)。空运单随货物一起送到目的港收货人手中。
- 发货人(托运人)。由航空公司签发给发货人，作为收货凭证，并作为发货人与航空公司之间的运输合约依据。

Shipper's Name and Address [shipper's Account Number] MATSUDA TELEVISION SYSTEMS CO. LOT5, PRESIAN TENKU APUAN SITE 400 SHA ALAM SELANG DE MALAYSIA						NOT NEGOTIABLE **Air Waybill** Issued by **Beijing Kinte World Express Co., ltd.**		
Consignee's Name and Address [Consignee's Account Number] MATSUDA QINGDAO CO., LTD. NO. 128 WUHAN ROAD QINGDAO CHINA						It is agreed that the goods described herein are accepted in apparent good order and condition (except as noted) for carriage SUBJECT TO THE CONDITIONS OF CONTRACT ON THE REVERSE HEREOF, ALL GOODS MAY BE CARRIED BY ANY OTHER MEANS. INCLUDING ROAD OR ANY OTHER CARRIER UNLESS SPECIFIC CONTRARY INSTRUCTIONS ARE GIVEN HEREON BY THE SHIPPER. THE SHIPPER'S ATTENTION IS DRAWN TO THE NOTICE CONCERNING CARRIER'S LIMITATION OF LIABILITY. Shipper may increase such limitation of liability by declaring a higher value of carriage and paying a supplemental charge if required.		
Issuing Carrier's Agent Name and City **Beijing Kinte World Express Co., ltd.**								
Agents IATA Code		Account No.						
Airport of Departure(Add. of First Carrier) and Requested Routing K.LUMPUR, MALAYSIA						Accounting Information FREIGHT COLLECT		
To QD	By first carrier KE	To	By	To	By	Currency USD	Declared Value for Carriage NVD	Declared Value for Customs NVD
Airport of Destination QINGDAO, CHINA		Flight/Date KE855/17JUN		Amount of Insurance		INSURANCE—If carrier offers insurance and such insurance is requested in accordance with the conditions thereof indicate amount to be insured in figures in box marked "Amount of Insurance".		
Handling Information "NOTIFY PARTY—SAME AS CONSIGNEE"								

No. of Pieces	Gross Weight	Rate Class	Chargeable Weight	Rate/Charge	Total	Nature and Quantity of Goods
52	510.00		211	AS ARRANGED		TV-PARTS 12.638M3

Prepaid Weight Charge Collect AS ARRANGED	Other Charges
Valuation Charge	
Tax	
Total Other Charges Due Agent	Shipper certifies that the particulars on the face hereof are correct and that insofar as any part of the consignment contains dangerous goods, such part is properly described by name and is in proper condition for carriage by air according to the applicable dangerous goods regulations. _____ Signature of Shipper or His Agent
Total Other Charges Due Carrier	
Total Prepaid	Total Collect AS ARRANGED	JUN. 10, 2020 QINGDAO KEWQAO
Currency Conversion Rates	CC Charges in des. Currency	Executed on____ at_____ Signature of issuing Carrier or as Agent
For Carrier's Use Only at Destination	Charges at Destination	Total Collect Charges	AIR WAYBILL NUMBER KEW-51000788

Figure 9-2　Air Waybill

图 9-2　空运单

As the goods go forward, an air waybill goes automatically to the consignee or customer and enables him to collect the goods without extra procedure, unless there is a **COD** arrangement. Such an arrangement is a major protection when using air freight if payment is required

COD
(cash on delivery)
abbr. 货到付款

当货物运出时，空运单便直接交给收货人或顾客，使他无须经过其他程序就能提到货物，除非事先有货到付款的安排。这种安排是因为收货人支付完货款才能提货，也是对发货人的一

before the goods are collected by the customer.

3. Commercial Invoice

The commercial invoice acts mainly as a record of the export transaction for buyers, sellers and customs authorities. Copies of the invoice are used by the exporters, their bank, the paying bank, the **receiving agents** at the port of discharge, the customs in the exporting country and the importers. The importers need it to **check up** whether the goods consigned to him are in compliance with the terms and conditions of the respective contract.

The banks need it together with the bill of lading and the insurance certificate to effect payment. The customs need it to calculate duties, if any. The exporters and importers need it to keep their accounts. In the absence of a draft, the commercial invoice takes its place for **drawing money**.

To understand and be able to write an invoice you should think about the following points (See Figure 9-3).

receiving agent
收货代理

check up
检查；核对

draw money
提款，取款

3. 商业发票

商业发票主要是为买方、卖方和海关当局提供一种出口交易的记录。出口商及其银行、付款行，卸货港的接收代理、出口国和进口国的海关都要使用商业发票。进口商用发票来检查所运达的货物是否与相应的合同中的条款一致。

银行需要用商业发票连同提单和保险单来进行议付。海关需要用商业发票来计算关税(如果有关税的情况)。出口商和进口商需要用商业发票来记账。在没有汇票的情况下，商业发票可以取代汇票来收取钱款。

为了理解并能拟定一份商业发票，应考虑以下要点(如图9-3所示)。

TENDAK DIGITAL TECHNOLOGY CO., LTD.

3F,Bldg B2,Hekan Industrial Park,Wuhe Rd S.,Longgang District,518028,Shenzhen,PRC
Tel: 86-755-82130281,82   Fax: 86-755-82130283
Web: www.z-tendak.com   E-mail: info@z-tendak.com

COMMERCIAL INVOICE

To: Shinsedai Co.,Ltd

400 Yamadera-cho,Kusatsu-City Shiga 525-8567 Japan

ATTN: Yoshiaki Nakanishi

TEL: 81-77-565-6050

Ref. No.: TD-T110921

Date: 2020/9/23

ITEM	Product Name	Trade Term	Sample Price (USD)	QTY (PCS)	Sub Total (USD)
TB-01	TV BOX 电视盒	FOB Shenzhen	75.00	2	150.00
	Total			2	150.0
SAY TOTAL USD ONE HUNDRED AND FIFTY ONLY.					

Note:

1. Shipped by DHL Express (AWB: 688 2079 186).

2. Package data: 1.2KGS, 25×18×10cm.

3. Origin: made in China.

4. For sample testing purpose, no real commercial value.

The Seller: _____

Figure 9-3 Commercial Invoice

图 9-3 商业发票

- seller's contact information;
- buyer's contact information;
- the invoice number (for your records);
- the order number;
- the reference number;
- the quantity and/or **description** of each item;
- the price of each item;
- the total price of items and total price of all items;
- the amount of discount allowed and the conditions;
- the method of freight, insurance and cost;
- the delivery address;
- the number of parcels, packages crates or other packing units;
- the markings on packing units.

4. Packing List

The packing list indicates the quantity of items in each package, along with their weight and dimension. Therefore the consignee is able to check and make sure that he receives the right quantity of items at destination. Customs authorities can also easily identify a specific package during custom inspection.

Packing list is a supplementary document for commercial invoice. It shows detail information about packing modes, packing materials, packing numbers, specification of cargo, quantities and weights, etc. There is no standard form for

description [dɪˈskrɪpʃən]
n. 描述；类型；说明书

- 卖方的联系信息；
- 买方的联系信息；
- 发票号(便于记录)；
- 订单号；
- 文档代码(参考编号)；
- 数量、各项商品的货名；
- 各项商品的价格；
- 各项商品的总价与所有商品的总价；
- 所同意的折扣数量及条件；
- 运费、保险费的结算方法及其价格；
- 发货地址；
- 包、件、箱或其他包装单元的数量；
- 包装单元上的标志。

4. 装箱单

装箱单标明了每一个包装内货物的数量、单件重量及尺寸，它便于收货人检查所到货物的数量的正确性，也方便海关清查时，能轻易地辨识出某一具体货物。

装箱单起到对商业发票内容的补充作用，它详细记载了包装方式、包装材料、包装数量及货物的规格、数量、重量等情况。装箱单并没有标准的格式，但通常包括出口商品名及地

the packing list, and **generally speaking**, it should include exporter's name and address, name and No. of document, shipping mark, name of commodity and specifications, quantity, unit, gross weight, net weight, measurement, signature. Below is a sample of packing list (See Figure 9-4).

generally speaking 一般而言

址、单据名称、装箱单编号、唛头、品名和规格、数量、单位、毛重、净重、尺码以及签名。装箱单样本如图 9-4 所示。

EXPORTER 公司英文名称 CONTACT: ALICE TELEPHONE: ×××			PACKING LIST		
IMPORTER ×××× CO.,LTD. 客户公司地址 Contact : ××× Telephone: ×××			P/L DATE:		
			INVOICE NO.:		
			INVOICE DATE:		
			CONTRACT NO.:		
Letter of Credit No.:			Date of Shipment:		
FROM:	Shanghai		TO:	Incheon	
Marks	Description of goods; Commodity No.	Quantity	Package	kg	kg	Meas.
N/M	×××	×××	××	××	500	1.2m³
	Total amount:	×××		××	500	1.2m³
			Exporter stamp and signature Alice			

Figure 9-4   Packing List

图 9-4   装箱单

5. Certificate of Origin

A Certificate of Origin is a document, required by foreign governments, declaring that goods in a particular international shipment are from a certain origin. Although the commercial invoice usually includes a statement of origin, some countries require a separate certificate for it. Customs offices will use this document to determine whether a preferential duty rate can **be applicable to** the products being imported, or whether a shipment can be legally imported during a specific **quota** period.

A Certificate of Origin is a signed statement issued by the country of origin for its exported products. The country of origin is not the country from where the product is shipped. The country of origin is the country where the product was manufactured or underwent **substantial** change or modification (See Figure 9-5).

For example, for 100% cotton, **knit** T shirts manufactured in China are shipped to the U.S. and have a logo or **slogan** placed on them, and were then shipped to **Poland**, the country of origin would be China. However, if the cotton knit fabric was manufactured in China and shipped to the U.S. and then the fabric was transformed into T shirts and T shirts were exported to Poland, the country of origin would be the U.S.

be applicable to 适应于，应用于
quota ['kwəutə]
n. 配额；定额；限额

substantial [səb'stænʃəl]
adj. 大量的；实质的
knit [nɪt]
vt. 编织
n. 针织衫
slogan ['sləugən]
n. 标语
Poland ['pəulənd]
n. 波兰(欧洲国家)

5. 原产地证明

原产地证明(书)是按外国政府的要求对在国际贸易运输中的货物说明其生产地或制造地的一个证明文件。尽管商业发票通常也有原产地声明，但有的国家规定还需单独的一份证明书。而海关也依靠这个文件确定某些进口产品是否适用优惠税率，某些产品的进口是否在特定的配额时期内是合法的。

原产地证明是一种签署的证明，说明某一装运出口产品的原产国。原产国并非指该产品的发运国，而是指产品的制造国或对产品进行过巨大改变或修整的国家(如图9-5所示)。

例如，某种在中国制造的纯棉针织T恤衫运往美国后，加贴标志又转口到波兰，此时这批T恤衫的原产国应是中国。然而，如果是在中国完成织布，运送到美国加工制成T恤衫，再出口到波兰，此时，这批T恤衫的原产国便是美国。

1.Exporter	Certificate No.
2.Consignee	**CERTIFICATE OF ORIGIN OF THE PEOPLE'S REPUBLIC OF CHINA**
3.Means of transport and route	5.For certifying authority use only
4.Country / Region of destination	

6.Marks and numbers	7.Number and kind of packages; description of goods	8.H.S.Code	9.Quantity	10.Number and date of invoices

11.Declaration by the exporter The undersigned hereby declares that the above details and statements are correct, that all the goods were produced in China and that they comply with the Rules of Origin of the People's Republic of China.	12.Certification It is hereby certified that the declaration by the exporter is correct.
-- Place and date, signature and stamp of authorized signatory	-- Place and date, signature and stamp of certifying authority

Figure 9-5　Certificate of Origin

图 9-5　原产地证明

Part 2　Letter of Credit　信用证

1. Concept of a Letter of Credit

A letter of credit is a written promise which is issued to the exporter by the opening or issuing bank upon the request of the applicant (the importer), promising a certain payment to a beneficiary (the exporter) against complying documents as stated in the letter of credit. Letter of credit is **abbreviated** as LC or L/C, and often is referred to as a **documentary credit**, abbreviated as DC or D/C.

When reading a letter of credit (See Table 9-1), we can find the main content of L/C including the follow information: destination bank, type of documentary credit, date and place of issue, date and place of expiry, applicant, beneficiary, advising bank, documents required, description of goods or services, and so on.

abbreviate
[ə'bri:vɪeɪt]
vt. 缩写

documentary credit
[金融] 押汇信用证，跟单信用证

2. The Parties Related to a L/C

- The applicant

It is generally the buyer or importer who applies to the bank for issuance of L/C.

- The beneficiary

The beneficiary under L/C is usually the seller or the exporter.

- The opening bank or issuing bank

It is the bank that issues the L/C on behalf of the applicant, and will be

1. 信用证的概念

信用证是基于申请者(进口方)的请求，由开证银行开给出口方的一份书面保证，如果有信用证，就能保证给受益人(出口方)一定数额的支付款。信用证可以缩写为 LC 或 L/C，经常涉及的是跟单信用证，缩写为 DC 或 D/C。

阅读信用证时(如表 9-1 所示)，会看到信用证的主要内容包括下列信息：目的地银行、跟单信用证的类型、开立的日期和地点、到期的日期和地点、申请者、受益人、通知行、要求的单据、货物或服务的描述等。

2. 信用证涉及的各方

- 申请人

一般指买方或进口商，它要求银行开立信用证。

- 受益人

信用证下的受益人通常指卖方或出口方。

- 开证行或出证行

代表申请人出证的银行，它通常要对付款负责任。卖方总是要求开证行为一级银行。

responsible for payment commonly. A first class bank is always being required as an opening bank by the seller.

- The advising bank

It is usually the exporter's local bank. The advising bank passes the L/C on to the beneficiary under the instruction from issuing bank and is not responsible for payment. It may be a branch of issuing bank or its correspondent.

- The negotiating bank

The negotiating bank is ready to pay for the drafts and get the full set of documents or only receive the drafts and documents without responsibility of payment, then mail them to the issuing bank for **reimbursement**. The negotiating bank may be the advising bank.

- The paying bank

The paying bank is responsible for the payment specified by the L/C. Usually it is the issuing bank or appointed by the issuing bank.

reimbursement
[ˌriːɪmˈbɜːsmənt]
n. 退还，偿还；赔偿

- 通知行

通常是出口方的当地银行。通知行按开证行的指令将信用证转给受益人，并不对付款负责。它通常是开证行的分行或相关银行。

- 议付行

议付行准备支付汇票并获得全套单据或只收汇票和单据不对付款负责，然后将这些单据寄给开证行付款。议付行可以是通知行。

- 付款行

付款行负责按信用证规定付款。通常它是开证行或开证行指定的银行。

Table 9-1 Specimen L/C

Issue of a Documentary Credit	BKCHCNBJA08E SESSION: 000 ISN: 000000 BANK OF CHINA LIAONING NO. 5 ZHONGSHAN SQUARE ZHONGSHAN DISTRICT DALIAN CHINA
Destination Bank	KOEXKRSEXXX MESSAGE TYPE: 700 KOREA EXCHANGE BANK SEOUL 178.2 KA, ULCHI RO, CHUNG-KO

(Continued)

Type of Documentary Credit	40A	IRREVOCABLE
Letter of Credit Number	20	LC84E0081/07
Date of Issue	31C	07072531D
Date and Place of Expiry	31D	070824 KOREA
Applicant Bank	51D	BANK OF CHINA LIAONING BRANCH
Applicant	50	DALIAN WEIDA TRADING CO., LTD
Beneficiary	59	SANGYONG CORPORATION CPO BOX 110　SEOUL　KOREA
Currency Code, Amount	32B	USD 1146725.04
Available with...by...	41D	ANY BANK BY NEGOTIATION
Drafts at	42C	45 DAYS AFTER SIGHT
Drawee	42D	BANK OF CHINA LIAONING BRANCH
Partial Shipments	43P	NOT ALLOWED
Transshipment	43T	NOT ALLOWED
Shipping on Board/Dispatch/Packing in Charge at/ from	44A	RUSSIAN BLACK SEA
Transportation to	44B	DALIAN PORT, P.R.CHINA
Latest Date of Shipment	44C	070820
Description of Goods or Services	45B	FROZEN YELLOWFIN USD770/MT CFR DALIAN QUANTITY: 200MT ALASKA PLAICE USD600/MT CFR DALIAN QUANTITY: 300MT

Documents Required:　　　　46

1. SIGNED COMMERCIAL INVOICE IN 5 COPIES.
2. FULL SET OF CLEAN ON BOARD OCEAN BILLS OF LADING MADE OUT TO ORDER AND BLANK ENDORSED, MARKED "FREIGHT PREPAID" NOTIFYING LIAONING OCEAN FISHING CO., LTD. TEL: (86)411-3680288
3. PACKING LIST/WEIGHT MEMO IN 4 COPIES INDICATING QUANTITY/GROSS AND NET WEIGHTS OF EACH PACKAGE AND PACKING CONDITIONS AS CALLED FOR BY THE L/C.
4. CERTIFICATE OF QUALITY IN 3 COPIES ISSUED BY PUBLIC RECOGNIZED SURVEYOR.
5. BENEFICIARY'S CERTIFIED COPY OF FAX DISPATCHED TO THE ACCOUNTEE WITH 3 DAYS AFTER SHIPMENT ADVISING NAME OF VESSEL, DATE, QUANTITY, WEIGHT, VALUE OF SHIPMENT, L/C NUMBER AND CONTRACT NUMBER.

(Continued)

6. CERTIFICATE OF ORIGIN IN 3 COPIES ISSUED BY AUTHORIZED INSTITUTION.

7. CERTIFICATE OF HEALTH/QUARANTINE IN 3 COPIES ISSUED BY AUTHORIZED INSTITUTION.

ADDITIONAL INSTRUCTIONS 47A

1. CHARTER PARTY B/L AND THIRD PARTY DOCUMENTS ARE ACCEPTABLE.
2. SHIPMENT PRIOR TO L/C ISSUING DATE IS ACCEPTABLE.
3. BOTH QUANTITY AND AMOUNT 10 PERCENT MORE OR LESS ARE ALLOWED.

Charges	71B	ALL BANKING CHARGES OUTSIDE THE OPENING BANK ARE FOR BENEFICIARY'S ACCOUNT.
Period for Presentation	48	DOCUMENTS MUST BE PRESENTED WITHIN 15 DAYS AFTER THE DATE OF ISSUANCE OF THE TRANSPORT DOCUMENTS BUT WITHIN THE VALIDITY OF THE CREDIT.
Confirmation Instructions	49	WITHOUT
Instructions to the Paying/Accepting/Negotiating Bank	78	1. ALL DOCUMENTS TO BE FORWARDED IN ONE COVER, UNLESS OTHERWISE STATED ABOVE. 2. DISCREPANT DOCUMENT FEE OF USD 50.00 OR EQUAL CURRENCY WILL BE DEDUCTED FROM DRAWING IF DOCUMENTS WITH DISCREPANCIES ARE ACCEPTED. THIS FEE SHOULD BE CHARGED TO THE BENEFICIARY.
"Advising Through" Bank	57A	KOREA EXCHANGE BANK SOUTH KOREA 178.2 KA, ULCHI RO, CHUNG-KO

表 9-1 信用证示例

开证行		中行辽宁分行 中国大连中山区中山广场 5 号
通知行		汉城韩国汇行 178.2 KA, ULCHI RO, CHUNG-KO
跟单信用证类型	40A	不可撤销
信用证号	20	LC84E0081/07
出证日期	31C	07072531D

续表

有效日期和有效地点	31D	070824 韩国
申请行	51D	中行辽宁分行
申请人	50	大连伟达贸易公司
受益人	59	韩国汉城 SANGYONG 公司
结算货币和金额	32B	USD 1146725.04
指定银行和信用证兑付方式	41D	任何银行议付有效
汇票付款期限	42C	45 天远期
受票人	42D	中行辽宁分行
分批装运	43P	不可
转船	43T	不可
装船、发送和货物接收监管的地点	44A	俄罗斯黑海
运至	44B	中国大连
最迟装运日期	44C	070820
货品说明	45B	冷冻黄鳍金枪鱼，成本加运费至大连每吨 770 美元 数量：200 吨 阿拉斯加欧蝶鱼，成本加运费至大连每吨 600 美元 数量：300 吨

所需单据： 46

1. 签字的商业发票五份。
2. 一整套清洁已装船提单，按指令和空白背书填制，且注明运费已付，通知人为辽宁海洋捕捞公司，电话：86-411-3680288。
3. 装箱单/重量单四份，显示每个包装产品的数量/毛净重和信用证要求的包装情况。
4. 由公认的检验人签发的质量证明三份。
5. 受益人证明的传真件，在船开后三天内将船名航次、日期、货物的数量、重量、价值、信用证号和合同号通知付款人。
6. 当局签发的原产地证明三份。
7. 当局签发的健康/检疫证明三份。

附加说明： 47A

1. 租船提单和第三方单据可以接受。
2. 装船期早于信用证的签发日期是可以接受的。
3. 允许数量和金额公差在 10%左右。

费用	71B	开证行以外的所有费用由受益人承担
出证日期	48	单证必须在运输单证出具后 15 天内出齐，而且在信用证有效期内
保兑指示	49	无

续表

对付款行、通知行、议付行的指示	78	1. 所有单证须一次性寄送,除非另外说明 2. 如果接受了有不符点的单证,不符点单证费50美元或同值的货币将由汇单中扣除。这一费用应由受益人承担
通知行	57A	韩国汇行 178.2 KA, ULCHI RO, CHUNG-KO

Summary 本章小结

The main functions of logistics documents are to provide a specific and complete description of goods so that they can be correctly processed for transport, payment, credit, import duty, etc. This chapter mainly deals with bill of lading, packing list, air waybill, commercial invoice, certificate of origin and L/C.

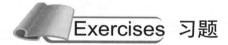

Exercises 习题

Questions for Review 复习题

1. What is the basic information shown on B/L?
2. How does air waybill take effect?
3. What is the function of commercial invoice?
4. If cotton knit fabric is manufactured in China and made to a T-shirt in USA, what is the origin of the shirt?
5. How does L/C take effect?

True or False 判断对错

1. A bill of lading is a document issued and signed by a shipper.
2. Letter of credit is abbreviated as LC or L/C, and often is referred to as a documentary credit, abbreviated as DC or D/C.
3. Air waybill is not a negotiable document and the shipper loses ownership of the goods after handing it over to the airline.
4. The commercial invoice acts mainly as a record of the export transaction for buyers, sellers and customs authorities.

5. A Certificate of Origin is a signed statement issued by the country of origin where the product is shipped out.

Case Study 案例分析题

Get a blank bill of lading from a forwarding agency or copy the bill of lading shown below. Fill in the details for the following transaction.

装货公司：Baumann Gabelstapler GmbH, Industry 5, D-25436 Tornesch
收货方：Constructa Development Corp., 77 Paramatta Road, Delhi, India
货运公司：Transworld Calcutta
货物：叉式装卸机备件
总重量：90 kg
规格：224 cm×45 cm×73 cm
专用箱：MAXU 2131718
目的港：Calcutta
送货点：Delhi
装货日期：2019 年 4 月 14 日
运费：预付运费
包装：木箱一个
价值：4150 欧元
运送港：Rotterdam
提单数量：3
货船：Indian Princess
预计抵达日期：2019 年 5 月 19 日
签发日期：2019 年 4 月 14 日

SHIPPER		B/L NO.
CONSIGNEE		**IN APPARENT GOOD ORDER ON BOARD B/L** ×××　OCEAN SHIPPING (GROUP) CO. ORINGINAL
NOTIFY PARTY		
PLACE OF RECEIPT	PORT OF LOADING	COMBINED TRANSPORT BILL OF LADING
PORT OF DISCHARGE	PLACE OF DELIVERY	
OCEAN VESSEL	VOYAGE NO.	

MARKS N/M	NOS. & KINDS OF PKGS	DESCRIPTION OF GOODS		G.W.(kg)	MEAS(CBM)
FREIGHT & CHARGES		IN WITNESS WHERE OF THE CARRIER OR HIS AGENT HAS SIGNED THE ABOVE STATED NUMBER OF BILL OF LADING ALL OF THIS TENOR AND DATE, ONE OF WHICH BEING ACCOMPLISHED THE OTHERS TO STAND VOID.			
TERMS AND CONDITIONS AS PER BACK HEREOF		PLACE OF ISSUE:			
		DATE OF ISSUE:			
		ON BOARD DATE:			
FREIGHT AND CHARGES		SIGNED (FOR THE MASTER) BY:			
NO. OF ORIGINAL B(s)/L		SIGNED FOR THE CARRIER:		SIGNATURE	

Chapter 10

Logistics Information Technology
物流信息技术

UPC(Universal Product Code)

通用商品码

When Marsh Supermarket store cashier Sharon Buchanan **scanned** a pack of **Wrigley**'s spearmint gum in 1974, she had no idea she was marking a technological **milestone**. "I don't think any of us realized at the time how far this was going. The fact is that we were first in the world. We had no idea that was going on either."

The rest, as they say, is history. Three decades later, the Universal Product Code — UPC for short — is **stamped** on everything from floral arrangements to home hardware. GS1 US, the organization that administers UPC. standards, estimates barcodes are scanned about 10 billion times a day around the world. GS1 President Michael Di Yeso says the technology, which was developed in the early 1970s by the U.S. grocery industry, is now used by manufacturers and retailers in more than 150 countries.

" I think it became obvious early on that as the scanning process took place and computers were capturing information, that information could be used beyond just price checks," he said. "They began to use that information for inventory control and

scan [skæn]
vt. 扫描；浏览

Wrigley ['rɪgli:]
n. 箭牌(口香糖品牌)

milestone ['maɪlstəun]
n. 里程碑，划时代的事件

stamp [stæmp]
v. 在……上印，盖印

1974 年，当 Marsh 超市的出纳员沙伦·布坎南扫描着一包箭牌薄荷味口香糖时，她不知道她正在树立一个技术里程碑。"我不认为我们当中有人认识到了这将会走得多远。事实上，我们是全球第一使用人，但我们也不知道究竟能继续走多远。"

其余的，正如他们所说，成为了历史。30 年后，通用产品码，简称 UPC，被广泛印贴在从植物盆景到五金产品上。美国 UPC 标准化组织 GS1 估计，在全球，每天大约有 100 亿次扫描条形码。GS1 主席迈克尔·迪·耶森说，该技术在 20 世纪 70 年代早期被用于美国的食品行业，现在，在全球 150 多个国家里，被应用于所有生产制造和零售等行业。

"我认为，这是很显而易见的，初期在电脑录入条形码扫描信息的过程中，人们就发现这些条形码信息

Chapter 10 Logistics Information Technology
物流信息技术

sharing that information back with their suppliers to improve availability of products on their **shelves**."

Although it took several years to gain acceptance, GS1 believes the system of 59 black and white bars has extended the space of commerce and saved consumers, all these make more than a **trillion** dollars. The system continues to evolve. Di Yeso says "Reduced Face **Symbology**", which reduces the barcodes to very small patterns, is now playing a major role in the health industry.

"The same technology that was invented 30 years ago that helped people move through the grocery line faster, is now saving lives in hospitals all across North America, but also in other parts of the world." he said.

In 2003, GS1 developed a new standard, the Electronic Product Code, which uses wireless technology and can transmit product information over the Internet.

"We believe very strongly that once the electronic product code begins to seed itself into retail, manufacturing, health care and other supply chains, the benefits of the electronic product code will provide, will **eclipse** the benefits from the UPC barcode that I talked about earlier, " Di Yeso said.

Whatever the future brings, the UPC's contributions to global commerce have already been immortalized in the

shelf [ʃelf]
n. 架子；搁板

trillion ['trɪljən]
adj. 万亿的

symbology [sɪm'bɒlədʒɪ]
n. 符号学，符号使用

eclipse [ɪ'klɪps]
vt. 使黯然失色

可以用于价格审核以外的领域。"他说。"他们开始将这些信息用于库存控制，同时与他们的供应商分享这些信息以提高生产计划的有效性。"

虽然花了几年时间去赢得大家的接受，但GS1相信，59条黑白条创造的商业空间和留住的客户超过了万亿美元。这个信息系统继续在发展完善。迪·耶森说，将条形码缩减呈现在非常小的样品上的"简化符号表示法"，今天在健康行业担任着主要角色。

"30年前发明的同样技术已经帮助人们提高食品生产线的效力，现在，正用于北美医院来救命，而且在全世界的其他地方也一样。"他说。

2003年，GS1创造了一个新的标准：电子产品码。它使用无线技术，同时能将产品信息发射至互联网。

"我们坚信，一旦电子产品码开始应用于零售业、制造业、卫生保健业和其他供应链，电子产品码提供的优势便会显现，届时，我之前所提到的UPC产品码的作用便会黯然失色。"迪·耶森说。

Smithsonian Museum of American History—along with a 30-year-old pack of chewing gum.

Smithsonian n. 史密森尼(美国博物馆)

这包 30 多年前的口香糖目前在美国史密森尼博物馆的历史馆展出。由此无论将来发生什么，通用商品码对全球商业的贡献已经名垂千古。

专栏 10-1　电子产品代码

电子产品代码是与全球标准代码条形码相对应的射频技术代码。电子产品代码由一系列数字组成，能够辨别具体对象的生产者、产品、定义，序列号。它除了具有全球标准代码能辨识物体的功能外，还可以通过电子产品代码网络提供关于产品的附加信息，例如产地、产品历史等，这些数据对于在供给链中特定产品的历史追踪具有关键的作用。这些数据被储存在互联网或其他网络上，只要使用标准的技术就可以进入数据系统，就像进入互联网一样。

Learning Objectives【学习目标】

- To understand the functions of logistics information system (LIS).
- To learn about usage of barcode and scanning technologies.
- To know the use of radio-frequency exchange technology.

Key Terms【关键词】

LIS	物流信息系统	scanning technology	扫描技术
barcode	条形码	auto ID	自动识别
RFDC	无线射频数据通信	RFID	无线射频识别

Part 1　Definition of LIS　物流信息系统的定义

Contemporary logisticians and supply chain managers must determine which data are relevant to their purposes, must organize and analyze these data, and then must act on them, and do so in as

contemporary [kən'tempərɪ] adj. 当代的；同时代的；属于同一时期的

现代物流和供应链管理人员必须确定哪些数据与他们的目标是相关的，必须收集并分析这些数据，并尽可能在短时间内依据这

Chapter 10 Logistics Information Technology
物流信息技术

short a time period as possible. So it's necessary for data management to support logistics management, and it has created demand for specialized information systems designed for logistics management needs. Many firms are beginning to better understand the need for logistics information support, and as a result, have begun to invest in technologies that enhance decision-making capabilities for transportation management, warehouse management, and demand forecasting and planning among others. Advanced technologies are used for **capturing** and communicating related logistics data, such as barcoding, electronic data interchange (EDI), and radio frequency identification (RFID).

Logistics information system(LIS)can be defined as "the people, equipment, and **procedures** to gather, sort, analyze, evaluate, and distribute needed, timely, and accurate information for logistics decision makers."

capture
['kæptʃə]
vt. 俘获；夺得

procedure
[prə'si:dʒə]
n. 程序；规程

些数据采取行动。所以，物流管理需要用数据管理加以支持，由此，针对物流管理而专门设计的信息系统应运而生。许多公司开始更好地理解需要物流信息支持的必要性，他们已经在技术上加大投资，以提高对于货物运输管理、仓储管理的决策能力，并且在计划和预测上提供资金。条形码、电子数据信息交换以及无线射频识别等先进技术被用来获取有关物流的信息并用于进行物流信息交换。

物流信息系统可以定义为"由人员、设备和程序组成的，通过收集、分类、分析、评估和分配信息数据，为物流决策者提供所需的、及时准确的信息的交互系统"。

Part 2   Barcode and Scanning Technologies 条形码及扫描技术

Auto Identification (ID) systems such as barcoding and electronic scanning were developed to facilitate logistics information collection and exchange. Typical applications include tracking warehouses receipts and retail sales. These ID systems require significant capital investment but replace the

自动识别(ID)系统，如条形码和电子扫描，能够促进物流信息的收集与交换。它主要用于追踪库存接收信息以及销售信息。建立一个自动识别系统需要进行大量的投资，但是这笔投资却非常值得。在传统模式中，企业利用纸质作为

traditional ones which are **error-prone** and time-consuming paper-based information collection and exchange processes. Hence it deserves to invest and is necessary for enterprises to develop and utilize auto ID systems. In fact, increased domestic and international competition is driving shippers, carriers, warehouses, wholesalers, and retailers to develop and utilize auto ID capability to compete in today's market place.

Auto ID allows supply chain members to quickly track and communicate movement details with high accuracy and **timeliness**, so it is fast becoming a fundamental service requirement for freight tracking by carriers. Both consumers and B2B customers expect to be able to track the progress of their shipment using the Web-based system offered by carriers such as United Parcel Service and FedEx.

Barcoding is the placement of computer-readable codes on items, cartons, containers, pallets, and even rail cars. Barcode development and applications are increasing at a very rapid rate. While the benefits are obvious, it is not clear which symbologies will be adopted as industry standards. Standardization and flexibility are desirable to accommodate the needs of a wide range of industries, but they also increase cost, making it more difficult for small-size and

error-prone
adj. 易于出错的

timeliness
['taɪmlɪnɪs]
n. 及时；好时机

媒介来收集和交换信息。这种方式既容易出错，又浪费了大量时间。自动识别系统能够取代上述传统模式，因此对于企业而言是十分必要的。事实上，随着国内外竞争的不断加剧，托运人、承运人、仓库、批发商、零售商都不得不开发并利用自动识别技术增强竞争力，在当今市场上谋得一席之地。

自动识别系统能够使供应链成员快速准确地跟踪运作过程中的各种详细信息，并且实现信息在各成员之间的传递。因此，当承运人对货物情况进行跟踪时，自动识别系统就成为一个必不可少的基本服务系统。无论是普通消费者还是B2B的消费者，他们都希望能够使用承运人提供的网络查询系统(如FedEx和UPS的网上查询系统)，对自身货物的状态进行跟踪和查询。

条形码技术，就是在商品、纸盒、集装箱、托盘或者机动轨道车上放置一个电脑可以读取代码的技术。目前，条形码技术已经得到了广泛的应用，同时在以非常快的速度不断地发展。条形码的优点十分明显，但是我们无法确定究竟哪一种代码将会成为行业的标准编码。为了满足所有

medium-size shippers, carriers, and receivers to implement standardized technologies. While continued **convergence** to common standards is likely, surveys indicate that select industries represented by major shippers will continue to use **proprietary** codes to maximize their competitive position.

Another key component of auto ID technology is the scanning process, which represents the eyes of a barcode system. A scanner optically collects barcode data and converts them to usable information. There are two types of scanners: handheld and fixed position. Each type can utilize contact or noncontact technology. Handheld scanners are either **laser guns** (noncontact) or wands (contact). Fixed position scanners are either automatic scanners (noncontact) or card readers (contact). Contact technologies require the reading device to actually touch the barcode. A contact technology reduces scanning errors but decreases flexibility. Laser gun technology is the most popular scanning technology currently in use, **outpacing** wands as the most widely installed technology.

Scanning technology has two major applications in logistics. The first is Point-of-Sale (POS) in retail stores. In addition to ringing up receipts for consumers, retail POS applications

convergence
[kən'vɜ:dʒəns]
n. [数] 收敛；会聚，集合

proprietary
[prə'praɪət(ə)rɪ]
adj. 所有的；专利的；私人拥有的

laser gun
激光枪

outpace
[aʊt'peɪs]
vt. 赶过；超过……速度

行业的需要，代码必须同时具备标准性和灵活性，但是这样会导致成本的增加。因此，对于中小型规模的发货人、承运人和收货人来说，采用标准的条形码技术就会变得更加困难。尽管使用统一标准的条形码技术已经成为大势所趋，然而有关调查却表明，以一些大型航运企业为代表的特定企业还是会继续使用它们自己的代码，以获得最大的竞争优势。

自动识别技术的另一个关键组件是扫描处理，这是条形码系统的"眼睛"。它利用扫描仪通过光学方式收集条形码中的数据，然后将数据转换成可用信息。扫描仪可以分为手提式扫描仪和固定式扫描仪两种。每一种扫描仪都可以利用接触式或非接触式的扫描技术。手提式扫描仪包括雷射枪(非接触式)和条形码读入器(接触式)两种，自动扫描仪(非接触式)与读卡机(接触式)则属于固定式扫描仪。接触式技术要求数据读取设备接触到条形码，这种技术能够减少扫描中的错误，但是限制了扫描的灵活性。雷射枪是当前最流行的一种扫描技术。目前它已经取代了条形码读入器，成为应用最为广泛的一项扫描技术。

provide accurate inventory control at the store level. POS allows precise tracking of each Stock Keeping Unit (SKU) sold and can be used to facilitate inventory replenishment. In addition to providing accurate re-supply and marketing research data, POS can provide more timely strategic benefits to all channel members.

The second logistics scanning application is for materials handling and tracking. Through the use of scanner guns, materials handlers can track product movement, storage location, shipments, and receipts. While this information can be tracked manually, it is very time-consuming and subject to error. Wider usage of scanners in logistical applications will increase productivity and reduce errors. The demand for faster and less error-prone scanning technology drives rapid changes in the marketplace for applications and technology.

扫描技术在物流方面主要有两个用途。一是用于零售店电子收款系统(POS)中。POS 不仅可以将顾客的货款收据记录下来，还能帮助零售店进行有效的库存控制，它能够准确地追踪每一个已售出的每种库存单位的所需情况并获得所需信息，从而有利于零售店制订补货计划。除了提供精确的供给与营销调查数据之外，POS 还能为所有渠道成员带来战略收益。

扫描技术在物流方面的另一种应用是对物料进行管理与跟踪。在扫描枪的帮助下，物料管理人员可以及时地了解产品的移动情况、存放地点、发货及收货情况。尽管这些信息也可以用手工方式记录下来，但是那样既浪费时间，又容易出错。扫描仪在物流领域中的应用相当广泛，这进一步促进了生产力的发展，减少了错误。企业需要更快、更准确的扫描技术，这种需求促进了市场中自动识别技术的迅速发展。

专栏 10-2　二维条形码简介及应用

（1）高密度编码，信息容量大：可容纳多达 1850 个大写字母或 2710 个数字或 1108 个字节，或 500 多个汉字，比普通条码信息容量高

Data Matrix

Maxi Code

Aztec Code

QR Code

Vericode

PDF417

Ultracode
Code 49

Code 16K

几十倍。

(2) 编码范围广：该条码可以把图片、声音、文字、签字、指纹等可以数字化的信息进行编码，用条码表示出来；此外，还可以用来表示多种语言文字；也可表示图像数据。

(3) 容错能力强，具有纠错功能：这使得在二维条码因穿孔、污损等引起局部损坏时，照样可以正确得到识读，损毁面积达 50%仍可恢复信息。

(4) 译码可靠性高：它比普通条码译码错误率百万分之二要低得多，误码率不超过千万分之一。

(5) 可引入加密措施：保密性、防伪性好。

(6) 成本低，易制作，持久耐用。

(7) 条码符号形状、尺寸大小比例可变。

(8) 二维条码可以使用激光或 CCD 阅读器识读。

Part 3　Radio-Frequency Exchange Technology 无线射频交换技术

Radio-frequency data communication (RFDC) technology is used within relatively small areas, such as distribution centers, to facilitate two-way information exchange. A major application is real-time communication with mobile operators such as **forklift** drivers and order selectors. RFDC allows drivers to have instructions and priorities updated on a real-time basis instead of using a hard copy of instructions printed hours earlier. Real-time or Wi-Fi transmissions guide work flow, offer increased flexibility and responsiveness, and can improve service using fewer resources. Logistics RFDC applications also include two-way communication for warehouse picking, cycle counts, and label printing.

forklift
['fɔːklɪft]
n. 铲车；堆高机；叉式升降机

无线射频数据通信技术(RFDC)能促进双向信息交换，它通常被用于相对较小的区域中，如配送中心等。应用 RFDC 的主要目的之一，是加强与工作地点不固定人员(如升降车司机和订货人员)的实时通信。RFDC 使司机可以随时获得最新的指示，而不用去看一本数小时前才刚刚印制的操作指示。实时沟通有助于企业对员工的工作进行指导，提高了作业流程的灵活性与响应性，同时可以利用较少的资源提高服务质量。RFDC 在物流领域的应用还包括在仓库的选择、库存的循环盘点以及标签印刷等方面实现双向通信。

Advanced RFDC capabilities in the form of two-way voice communication are finding their way into logistics warehouse applications. Instead of requiring warehouse operations personnel to interface with a mobile or handheld computer, voice RFDC prompts operators through tasks with **audible** commands and waits for verbal responses or requests. United Parcel Service uses speech-based RFDC to read **zip codes** from incoming packages and print routing tickets to guide packages through their sortation facilities. The voice recognition systems are based on keywords and voice patterns of each operator. The primary benefit of voice-based RFDC is an easier operator interface; since keyboard data entry is not required, two hands are available for order picking.

Radio-frequency identification (RFID) is a second form of radio-frequency technology. RFID can be used to identify a container or its contents as it moves through facilities or on transportation equipment. RFID places a coded electronic **chip** in the container or box. RFID chips can be either active or passive. Active chips continuously emanate radio waves so that products can be located in a warehouse or a retail store, using receivers located throughout the store. Active chip technology is good for

audible [ˈɔːdɪb(ə)l]
adj. 听得见的

zip codes
邮政编码

chip [tʃɪp]
n. 碎片；[电子] 集成电路片

先进的 RFDC 即双向语音通信技术可以应用于物流的仓储管理中。应用了双向语音技术后，仓库管理员不需要使用手机或者手提电脑，能够直接用语音命令指示工作人员完成任务，然后等待工作人员做出回答。UPS 就利用这种具有语音功能的 RFDC 技术来读取包裹上的邮政编码，并打印出路线标签，指导如何对包裹进行下一步的分类。语音辨认系统的工作原理是：它通过识别关键词及辨认各个工作人员的声音特点来完成工作。语音 RFDC 的最大优点在于它非常简单实用。使用了具有语音功能的 RFDC 之后，工作人员不再需要用键盘输入数据，那么，他们的双手就可以被解放出来去进行订单的分拣工作了。

无线射频识别(RFID)技术是另一种无线射频技术。当一个集装箱在多个设施中进行处理，或者装载在运输设备上时就可以用 RFID 技术来确定集装箱所处的位置和它的容量。RFID 技术在集装箱或箱子中放入了一枚经过编码的电子芯片，这种芯片可以分为两类，活跃的和不活跃的。活跃的芯片不断地发射出无线电波，当我们用接收装置获取电波之后，就可以知道产品是在仓库中，还是位于零售商

locating product in a **facility** as well as for identifying when it is moving in and out of the facility. Passive chips respond only when they are electronically **stimulated** by having the product pass through a relatively small gateway or portal that has scanners built in. Since the product must be passed through a gateway for passive chips to operate, these can be used only for tracking product movement in, out, and around a facility. With current technology, the cost of active chips (GEN II) is approximately 10 times that of passive chips because of the need for a battery and larger **antenna**. As the container or box moves through the supply chain, it can be scanned for an identifying code or even for the list of contents. Retailers are beginning to use RFID to allow entire cartloads of RFID tags on their cases to facilitate processing in distribution warehouses, receipt at stores, and shelf restocking. While the benefits were apparent for the retailers, they were not so evident for the manufacturers, particularly since the retailers were not generally willing to pay for the chip and the technologies to employ it. While the initiatives to use RFID to track activity for consumer products have declined, there is significant application space for the use of RFID to enhance security and minimize counterfeiting. For example, there is increasing use of

facility [fə'sɪlɪtɪ]
n. 设施；设备

stimulate ['stɪmjʊleɪt]
vt. 刺激；鼓舞，激励

antenna [æn'tenə]
n. [电讯] 天线

店中。通过这种技术，我们不但可以确定产品的位置，还可以了解到产品于何时进入或离开某个设施。与之相比，只有用扫描仪进行扫描，刺激了芯片中的电子元器件之后，不活跃的芯片才会有所反应。正因为这样不活跃的芯片技术通常只用于跟踪产品进入、离开或停留在某设施中的状态信息。在当前的科技水平下，活跃芯片的成本(GEN II)几乎是不活跃芯片成本的10倍，这是因为制造活跃芯片时需要使用电池和大量的天线。当集装箱或箱子在供应链中流动时，我们可以通过扫描获得它们的编码信息，甚至知道箱子里装了哪些物品。零售商正在逐步使用RFID技术，他们允许(供应商)在货物上贴上RFID标签，以便能够(一次性)完成整车商品的扫描工作，从而简化产品分销、产品接收以及重新调整货架等工作。尽管对零售商来说采用射频技术的好处显而易见，然而对制造商来说采用射频技术的优势却并不那么明显。而且大部分零售商都不愿意为射频技术中用到的芯片和其他相关技术买单。因此为了跟踪客户所订购产品而应用射频技术的这种做法对企业来说不大有吸引力。但在加强产品的安全性、尽量杜绝仿冒产品方面，射频技术还是有很大的

RFID for **pharmaceuticals** and expensive technology to reduce counterfeiting and enhance security. It is anticipated that the lessons learned through these applications will reduce the price of RFID and will lead to future logistics applications.

pharmaceutical
[ˌfɑːməˈsuːtɪk(ə)l; -ˈsjuː-]
n. 药物

应用空间。比如，在制药业和高档科技产品制造业，应用射频技术的企业越来越多。我们可以推测，随着射频技术的运用越来越广泛，掌握射频技术应用知识的企业越来越多，射频技术的应用成本将不断降低，并将在未来的物流运作中得到广泛的应用。

Summary 本章小结

This chapter provides an overview of logistics information technology, emphasizes the importance of effective and efficient utilization of information for logistics management, especially lists the two advanced technologies of logistics information systems that are applicable across each business function－barcode technology and radio-frequency exchange technology.

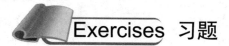

Questions for Review 复习题

1. What is logistics information system?
2. What is EDI?
3. What is a barcode?
4. What do you know about the applications of barcode technology in our daily life?

True or False 判断对错

1. In the logistics information system, EDI plays the most important role.
2. The logistics network is virtual network.
3. EDI provides for the seamless transmission of data across companies.
4. A barcode encoding scheme is represented only by numbers.
5. The adoption of barcodes can help both consumers and retailers to save money.

Chapter 10 Logistics Information Technology
物流信息技术

Topic for Discussion 讨论话题

Give the full names of the following:
LIS
EDI
RFID
UPC
AIDC
ASCII

Logistics English Dialogue 物流英语对话

Difference between Legacy System and Present System

(A, a logistical manager with rich experience in information management, is now talking in his office with Mr. B, a client who wishes to get acquainted with information system.)

B: Hello! Sorry to trouble you.

A: Never mind. Welcome to our company.

B: Today I would like to know something about the difference between legacy system and present system on information management.

A: Oh! It's like this. Legacy systems are older information systems based on mainframe technology that usually work at an operation level on only one stage or even one function within a stage of the supply chain.

B: What's the advantage of the present system ERP?

A: Enterprise resource planning(ERP), systems are operational information systems that gather information from across all of a company's functions, resulting in the entire enterprise having a broader scope.

B: A broader scope?

A: Yeah! Legacy systems can range from order entry to manufacturing scheduling to delivery, but present systems' scope allows ERP systems to track orders through the entire company from procurement to delivery.

B: Does that mean legacy systems tend to focus solely on a particular function and are built as independent entities with little regard for other systems?

A: That's it! For instance, a legacy system might deal only with inventory levels in a particular warehouse in a distributor's network. This system would monitor inventory levels in that warehouse, but would likely have difficulty communication with the legacy system that handled transportation for the same distributor; ERP systems monitor material, orders, schedules, finished goods inventory, and other information throughout the entire organization.

B: Thank you. Now I feel I know something about the legacy system and present system.

A: It's my pleasure. If you have any more questions about it, don't hesitate to let me know.

B: Sure, I will. See you later.

A: See you later.

Case Study 案例分析题

Electronic Data Interchange In the Port of Hamburg

Dakosy is a Hamburg-based company that provides data communication systems for the transport industry. Dakosy is one of the leading software developers for international freight forwarding and customs clearance. In conjunction with their subsidiary company, CargoSoft GmhH, Dakosy has a very strong market presence in international freight forwarding (sea and air). Dakosy AG also provides software solutions for clearing dangerous goods and for the needs of carriers. All of Dakosy's software solutions can be easily integrated into the IT systems of companies through open interfaces, where Dakosy's solutions can help companies to optimize their existing internal processes and make it possible for companies to execute electronic business transactions.

As a system vendor and clearance centre, Dakosy AG provides a wide range of IT and data centre services for their customers. More than 1 600 companies across Europe use Dakosy AG's state-of-the-art data centres for their electronic business communication. These companies include world famous trading houses, branded companies, industrial enterprises, freight forwarders, shipping companies, liner agents, carriers and various authorities (customs, harbour police and so on).

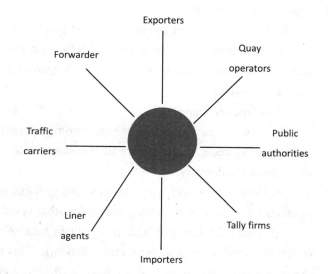

Discussion: Read the passage about the company and explain the meaning of the picture taken from Dakosy's brochure.

Appendix: Logistics Vocabularies 物流词汇

A

ABC classification ABC 分类法
a circular letter 通告信/通知书
accomplish a bill of lading (to) 付单提货
acquisition cost ordering cost 订货费
act of God 天灾
activity cost pool 作业成本集
activity-based costing 作业基准成本法
actual displacement 实际排水量
ad valorem freight 从价运费
addendum (to a charter party) (租船合同)附件
additional for alteration of destination 变更卸货港附加费
additional for optional destination 选卸港附加费
address commission (add comm) 回扣佣金
adjustment 海损理算
advance B/L 预借提单
advance shipping notice (ASN) 预先发货通知
a fixed day sailing 定日航班
a fortnight sailing 双周班
a Friday sailing 周五班
agile manufacturing 敏捷制造
air express 航空快递
airline operator/freight forwarder 不营运船舶的多式联运经营人
air waybill 航空运单
alliance 联盟
all in rate 总运费率
all purposes (A.P.) 全部装卸时间
all time saved (A.T.S.) 节省的全部时间
allocation 分配

always afloat 始终保持浮泊

American Bureau of Shipping (A.B.S.) 美国船级社

a monthly sailing 每月班

AMT (advanced manufacturing technology) 先进制造技术

anchorage 锚地

anchorage dues 锚泊费

annual survey 年度检验

anticipation inventory 预期储备

anti-dated B/L 倒签提单

APICS (American Production and Inventory Control Society, Inc.) 美国生产与库存管理系统

applied manufacturing education series 实用制造管理系列培训教材

apron 码头前沿

arbitration award 仲裁裁决

arbitrator 仲裁员

area differential 地区差价

arrest a ship 扣押船舶

AS/RS (automated storage/retrieval system) 自动化仓储系统

assemble-to-order 订货组装

assembly 组配，装配

article reserves 物品储备

ATP (available to promise) 可供销售量

automatic replenishment (AR) 自动补货系统

automatic warehouse 自动化仓库

automatic guided vehicle (AGV) 自动导引车

automated high-rise warehouse 自动立体仓库

average adjuster 海损理算师

average bond 海损分摊担保书

average guarantee 海损担保书

a weekly sailing 周班

axle housing 桥壳

axle load 轴负荷

B

backflushing 反冲法

backfreight 回程运费
back-hauls 回程空载
back (return) load 回程货
backlog 拖欠订单
back order 脱期订单，延期交货成本(back order costs)
back scheduling 倒排计划
back to back charter 转租合同
ballast (to) 空载行驶
bale or bale capacity 货舱包装容积
balse 包件
band conveyor 皮带运送机
barcode 条形码
bareboat (demise) charter party 光船租船合同
barge 驳船
barratry 船员不轨行为
barrel 琵琶桶
barrel handler 桶抓
base cargo 垫底货
base port 基本港，起运货量
batch process 批流程
bay number 排数
bay plan 预配图/集装箱船积载图(表)
beam 船宽
bearer (of a B/L) 提单持有人
bearer B/L 不记名提单
bill of lading 提单
bill of materials 物料清单
blank endorsement 空白背书
boarding agent / clerk 代理外勤(登轮)
boatman 缆工
body 车身
body shell 车身壳体
bottleneck 瓶颈资源(工序)
bonded area 保税区

bonded goods (goods in bond) 保税货物
bonded warehouse 保税仓库
book space 洽订舱位
booking agent the party who secures FOB cargo 订舱代理
booking note 托运单(定舱委托书)
boom of a fork-lift truck 铲车臂
booking number 订舱号
BOR (bill of resource) 资源清单
both ends (BENDS) 装卸两港
both to blame collision clause 互有过失碰撞条款
bottom 船底
bottom stow cargo 舱底货
bottomry loan 船舶抵押贷款
box 盒子
BP (base port) 基本港
box car 箱式车
brake 制动器
braking system 制动系
break-bulk 拆分
breakbulk 零担
breakbulk cargo 零担货物
breakage-proof 防破损
broken stowage 亏舱
brokerage 经纪人佣金
bucketless system 无时段系统
buffer stock 调节库
bulk cargo 散装货
bulk carrier 散货船
bulk container 散货集装箱
bundle (BD) 捆(包装单位)
bunker adjustment factor (surcharge) (BAS or BS) 燃油附加费
bunker escalation clause 燃料涨价条款
buoy 浮标
Bureau Veritas (B.V.) 法国船级社

business logistics 企业物流
business plan 经营规划
bunker supplier 船舶燃料供应公司

C

cable/telex release 电放
cabotage 沿海运输
CAD (computer-aided design) 计算机辅助设计
CAM (computer-aided manufacturing) 计算机辅助制造
can/tin 罐装，听装
canal transit dues 运河通行税
cancellation 退关箱
canvas 帆布
CAO (computer assisted ordering) 计算机辅助订货系统
capacity level 能力利用水平
capacity management 能力管理
capacity requirements planning 能力需求计划
capital payoff 投资回收
CAPP (computer-aided process planning) 计算机辅助工艺设计
capsize vessel 超宽型船
captain 船长
car carrier 汽车运输船
car container 汽车集装箱
cargo availability at destination 货物运抵目的地
cargo canvassing 揽货
cargo hook 货钩
cargo manifest 载货清单(货物舱单)
cargo sharing 货载份额
cargo superintendent 货物配载主管
cargo tank 货箱
cargo tracer 短少货物查询单
cargo under custom's supervision 海关监管货物
cargoworthiness 适货

carrying cost 保管费
carryings 运输量
carton 纸板箱，纸箱
cask 桶
casket 小箱
case 箱
CASE (computer-aided software engineering) 计算机辅助软件工程
centre of gravity 重心点
centre of gravity offset 重心偏斜
certificate of seaworthiness 适航证书
cesser clause 责任终止条款
CFS/CFS (S/S) 站到站
CFS/CY (S/Y) 站到场
channel of distribution 分销渠道
chargeable weight 计费重量
charter party (C/P) 租船合同(租约)
charter party B/L 租约项下提单
chartered carrier 包机运输
chassis 集装箱拖车，底盘
chest 箱
chill space 冷藏区
CIMS (computer integrated manufacturing system) 计算机集成制造系统
claims adjuster 理赔人
classification certificate 船级证书
classification register 船级公告
classification society 船级社
classification survey 船级检验
clean (petroleum) products 精炼油
clean B/L 清洁提单
clean the holds (to) 清洁货舱
closed-loop MRP 闭环 MRP
closing date 截止日
closure of navigation 封航
clutch 离合器

coastal transport 沿海运输
COD (change of destination) 更改目的地(改港)
coil 捆，盘装
cold chain 冷链
collapsible flattrack 折叠式板架集装箱
collective packing 组合包装
combination of rate 分段相加运价
combined transport 联合运输
commodity classification rates (CCR) 等价货物运价
commodity inspection 进出口商品检验
common carrier 公共承运人
common feeder 公共支线
COMMS (customer oriented manufacturing management system) 面向客户制造管理系统
competitors 竞争对手
completely knocked down (CKD) 全拆装
component 子件/组件
compulsory pilotage 强制引航
computer assisted ordering(CAO) 计算机辅助订货系统
conference 公会
conference carrier 公会承运人
congestion 拥挤
congestion surcharge 拥挤费
con-ro ship 集装箱/滚装两用船
consecutive single trip (C/P) 连续单航次租船合同
consecutive voyages 连续航程
consign 托运
consignee 收货人
consignment 托运；托运的货物
consignor 发货人
consolidation 集中托运
consolidation (groupage) 拼箱
consortium 联营
constants 常数
construction rate 比例运价

container 集装箱
container barge 集装箱驳船
container loading list 集装箱装船报
container straddle carrier 集装箱跨运
container freight station (CFS) 集装箱货运站
container leasing 集装箱租赁
container load plan 集装箱装箱单
container terminal 集装箱码头
container transport 集装箱运输
container yard (CY) 集装箱堆场
containers moving over the road 集卡
containerized 已装箱的，已集装箱化的
containerization 集装箱化
containership 集装箱船
contamination (of cargo) 货物污染
continuous process 连续流程
continuous replenishment program (CRP) 连续补充库存计划
contract logistics 合同物流
contract of affreightment (COA) 包运合同
contributory value 分摊价值
control device 控制装置
controlled carrier 受控承运人
conventional container ship 集装箱两用船
conveyor 输送机
conveyor belt 传送带
corner casting (fitting) 集装箱(角件)
corner post 集装箱(角柱)
corrosive 腐蚀性物品
cost driver 作业成本发生因素
cost driver rate 作业成本发生因素单位费用
costed BOM 成本物料单
cost of stockout 短缺损失
cost roll-up 成本滚动计算法
couriers UPS/TNT/HDS/EMS 快递

Appendix: Logistics Vocabularies
物流词汇

crane 起重机
crawler mounted crane 轨道式起重机
crank-connecting rod mechanism 曲柄连杆机构
crate 板条箱
crew list 船员名册
critical path method 关键路线法
critical ratio 紧迫系数
critical work center 关键工作中心
cross docking 交叉配送(换装)
cumulative lead time 累计提前期
currency adjustment factor (CAF) 货币贬值附加费
current standard cost 现行标准成本
custom of the port (COP) 港口惯例
customary assistance 惯常协助
customary quick despatch (CQD) 习惯快速装运
customer deliver lead time 客户交货提前期
customized logistics 定制物流
customization logistics 定制物流
customs broker 报关行
customs declaration 报关
cut-off time (latest possible time the cargo may be delivered to) 截关
cutting stock 下料
cycle counting 循环盘点
cycle stock 订货处理周期
CY/CY (Y/Y) 场到场
CY/CFS (Y/S) 场到站

D

daily running cost 日常营运成本
damage for detention 延期损失
dangerous cargo list 危险品清单
dangerous when wet 遇水燃烧品
days offset 偏置天数

DCS (distributed control system) 分布式控制系统
dead weight cargo tonnage (DWCT) 净载重吨
deadfreight 亏舱费
deadweight (weight) cargo 重量货
deadweight cargo (carrying) capacity 载货量
deadweight tonnage (all told) (DWT or D.W.A.T) 总载重吨位(量)
deadweight scale 载重图表
decision support system 决策支持系统
deck cargo 甲板货
declaration of ship's deadweight tonnage of cargo 宣载通知书
declared value for carriage 运输声明价值
declared value for customs 海关声明价值
delivery of cargo (a ship) 交货(交船)
delivery order (D/O) 提货单(小提单)
demand cycle 需求周期
demand management 需求管理
demonstrated capacity 纪实能力
demurrage 滞期费
demurrage half despatch (D1/2D) 速遣费为滞期费的一半
dependent demand 相关需求件
derrick 吊杆
despatch or despatch money 速遣费
destuff 卸集装箱
Det Norske Veritas (D.N.V.) 挪威船级社
deviation 绕航
deviation surcharge 绕航附加费
direct additional 直航附加费
direct B/L 直航提单
direct discharge (车船)直卸
direct store delivery(DSD) 店铺直送
direct transshipment 直接转船
dirty(black) (petroleum) products (D.P.P.) 原油
disbursements 港口开支
discharging port 卸货港

discrete manufacturing 离散型生产
dispatch list 派工单
dispatching planning 调度计划
disponent owner 二船东
distribution 配送
distribution centre(DC) 配送(分拨)中心
distribution logistics 销售物流，生产企业、流通企业出售商品时，物品在供方之间的实体流动
distribution processing 流通加工
distribution requirement planning(DRP Ⅰ) 配送需求计划
distribution resource planning (DRP Ⅱ) 配送资源计划，分销资源计划
DMRP (distributed MRP) 分布式 MRP
dock 船坞
dock receipt 场站收据
docker 码头工人
door to door 门到门运输
double-girder crane model with manual/electric hoist 手动葫芦
downtime (设备)故障时间
draft (draught) 吃水；水深
draft limitation 吃水限制
drive axle 驱动桥
dropping outward pilot (D.O.P.) 引航员下船时
drop and pull transport 甩挂运输
drop shipment 直运
drum 圆桶
dry cargo 干货
dry cargo (freight) container 干货集装箱
dry dock 干船坞
DTF (demand time fence) 需求时界
dunnage and separations 垫舱和隔舱物料

E

earliest due date 最早订单完成日期
ECO (engineering change order/notice) 技术变更通知

ECR (efficient customer response) 有效客户反应
EDI (electronic data interchange) 电子数据交换
engineering BOM 工程物料清单
engine body 机体
ETO (engineer-to-order) 专项生产
economic order quantity(EOQ) 经济订货批量
efficient deck hand (E.D.H.) 二级水手
electronic order system (EOS) 电子订货系统
elevator 卸货机
enter a ship inwards (outwards) 申请船舶进港(出港)
enterprise resource planning (ERP) 企业资源计划
entrepot 保税货
environmental logistics 绿色物流；环保物流
ergonomics 工效学
EOQ (economic order quantity) 经济定货量法
equipment 设备(常指集装箱)
equipment handover charge 设备使用费
equipment interchange receipt (EIR) 集装箱设备交接单
equipment utilization 设备利用率
estimated time of completion (ETC) 预计完成时间
estimated time of departure (ETD) 预计离港时间
estimated time of readiness (ETR) 预计准备就绪时间
estimated time of sailing (ETS) 预计航行时间
Europallet 欧式托盘
even if used (E.I.U.) 即使使用
excepted period 除外期间
exception 异议
exceptions clause 免责条款
excess landing 溢卸
expiry of laytime 装卸期满
explosive 爆炸品
export supervised warehouse 出口监管仓库
extend a charter 延长租期
extend suit time 延长诉讼时间

extension of a charter 租期延长
extension to suit time 诉讼时间延长
external logistics 社会物流，企业外部的物流活动的总称
extreme breadth 最大宽度

F

FAS (final assembly schedule) 总装进度
fairway 航道
favorable variance 有利差异
FCS (finite capacity scheduling) 有限能力计划
feature 特征件
feeder service 支线运输服务
feeder ship 支线船
ferry 渡轮
financial accounting 财务会计
financial entity 财务实体
finite forward scheduling 有限顺排计划
finite loading 有限排负荷
firm-planned order 确定订单
firm-planned time fence 确定计划时单
first class ship 一级船
fixed-interval system (FIS) 定期订货方式
fixed period requirements 定期用量法
fixed-quantity system (FQS) 定量订货方式
fixture note 租船确认书
flag of convenience (FOC) 方便旗船
flatbed 拖车
flatcar 平板车
floating crane 浮吊
floating dock 浮坞
floor stock 作业现场库存
flow of exchange 商流
flow of material 物流

flow of cash 资金流

FMS (flexible manufacturing system) 柔性制造系统

fork lift truck 叉车

force majeure 不可抗力

forklift 叉车，叉式升降装卸车

fork-lift truck 铲车

formal system 规范化管理系统

form utility 形状效用

forward scheduling 顺排计划

FOQ (fixed order quantity) 固定批量法

forty foot equivalent unit (FEU) 四十英尺集装箱换算单位

four-way pallet 四边开槽托盘

fragile 易碎品

frame 车架

franchised outlet 加盟店

free in (FI) 船方不负责装费

free in and out (FIO) 船方不负责装卸费

free in and out, stowed and trimmed (FIOST) 船方不负责装卸、理舱和平舱费

free out (FO) 船方不负责卸费

freeboard 干舷

freeze space 冷冻区

freight all kinds (FAK) 包干运费

freight canvasser 揽货员

freight claim 货物赔偿的要求

freight collect (freight payable at destination) 运费到付

freight manifest 运费舱单

freight prepaid 运费预付

freight quotation 运费报价

freight rate (rate of freight) 运费率

freight tariff 运费费率表

freight ton (FT) 运费吨

freighter 货船

fresh water load line 淡水载重线

Fridays and holidays excepted (F.H.E.X.) 星期五和节假日除外

front axle 前轴
fuel supply system 供给系
full and complete cargo 满舱满载货
full and down 满舱满载
full container load (FCL) 整箱货
full container ship 全集装箱船
full-load 满载
full-service distribution company (FSDC) 全方位物流服务公司
fumigation charge 熏蒸费

G

gantry crane 门式起重机(门吊)
gear box 变速器
Gencon 金康航次租船合同
general average 共同海损
general average act 共同海损行为
general average contribution 共同海损分摊
general average sacrifice 共同海损牺牲
general cargo (generals) 杂货
general cargo rates (GCR) 普通货物运价
general purpose container 多用途集装箱
geographical rotation 地理顺序
georgraphical information system (GIS) 地理信息系统
Germanischer Lloyd (G.L.) 德国船级社
global positioning system (GPS) 全球定位系统
goods collection 集货
goods shed 料棚
goods shelf 货架
goods stack 货垛
goods yard 货场
grabbing crane 抓斗起重机
Grain capacity 散装舱容
Greenwich Mean Time (G.M.T.) 格林威治时间

gross dead weight tonnage 总载重吨位
gross registered tonnage (GRT) 注册(容积)总吨
gross requirements 毛需求
gross weight(GW) 毛重
grounding 触底
GT (group technology) 成组技术
gunny bag 麻袋
gunny matting 麻垫

H

Hague Rules 海牙规则
Hague-visby Rules 海牙维斯比规则
Hamburg Rules 汉堡规则
hand hook 手钩
handle with care 小心轻放
handling/carrying 搬运
handymax 杂散货船
handy-sized bulker 小型散货船
harbour 海港
harbour dues 港务费
hatch (hatch cover) 舱盖
hatchway 舱口
head charter (charter party) 主租船合同
head charterer 主租船人
heavy fuel oil (H.F.O.) 重油
heavy lift 超重货物
heavy lift additional (surcharge) 超重附加费
heavy lift derrick 重型吊杆
heavy weather 恶劣天气
hedge inventory 囤积库存
high density cargo 重货
hire statement 租金单
hold 船舱

home port 船籍港
homogeneous cargo 同种货物
hook 吊钩
hopper 漏斗
house air waybill (HAWB) 航空分运单
house B/L 运输代理行提单
hovercraft 气垫船
husbandry 维修
humldity controlled space 控湿储存区
hyper production style 混合生产

I

ice-breaker 破冰船
identity of carrier clause 承运人责任条款
idle (船舶、设备)闲置
idle formality 例行手续
idle material 呆料
ignition system 点火系
immediate rebate 直接回扣
import entry 进口报关
in apparent good order and condition 外表状况良好
in bulk 散装化
indicative mark 指示性标志
indemnity 赔偿
indented BOM 缩排式物料清单
independent demand 独立需求
inducement 起运量
inducement cargo 起运量货物
infinite loading 无限排负荷
inflammable 易燃品
inflammable gas 易燃气体
inflammable solid 易燃固体
inflammable liquid 易燃液体
inflation adjustment factor (IAF) 通货膨胀调整系数

informal system 非规范化管理
infrastructure (of a port) (港口)基础设施
inherent vice 固有缺陷
inland container depot 内陆集装箱
input/output control 投入/产出控制
inspection 检验
Institute Warranty Limits (IWL) (伦敦保险人)协会保证航行范围
insufficient packing 包装不足
intaken weight 装运重量
integrated logistics 综合物流
intermodal transportation 多式联运，联合运输
International Air Transport Association (IATA) 国际航空运输协会
International Association of Classification Societies (IACS) 国际船级社协会
International Civil Aviation Organization (ICAO) 国际民用航空组织
International Maritime Dangerous Goods Code (IMDG) 国际海上危险品货物规则(国际危规)
International Maritime Organization (IMO) 国际海事组织
international multimodal transport 国际多式联运
international through railway transport 国际铁路联运
International Transport Workers' Federation (ITF) 国际运输工人联合会
internal logistics 企业物流
international logistics 国际物流
in-transit inventory 在途库存
inventory 库存
inventory control 存货控制
inventory cycle time 库存周期
inventory turnover/turns 库存(资金)周转次数
inward 进港的
inward cargo 进港货物
itinerary 航海日程表
item, material, part 物料
item master, material master 物料主文件

J

job shop 机群式布置车间

jettison 抛货
just in time(JIT) 准时制
just-in-time logistics 准时制物流
joint service 联合服务
joint distribution 共同配送
joint survey 联合检验
jumbo derrick 重型吊杆
jurisdiction (litigation) clause 管辖权条款

K

keep upright 勿倒置
keep in a dry place 在干燥处保管
keep in a cool place 低温保管
keep away from boilers 远离锅炉
keep away from heat 请勿受热
keep away from cold 请勿受冷
keep dry 防湿
kecp away fom moisture 怕湿
kitting 配套出售件
knot 航速(节)

L

labor productivity 劳动生产率
laden 满载的
laden draught 满载吃水
land bridge 陆桥
land bridge transport 大陆桥运输
landing charges 卸桥费
landing, storage and delivery 卸货、仓储和送货费
lash 用绳绑扎
lashings 绑扎物
latitude 纬度

laydays (laytime) 装卸货时间
lay up 搁置不用
lay-by berth 候载停泊区
laydays canceling (laycan 或 L/C) 销约期
laytime saved 节省的装卸时间
laytime statement 装卸时间计算表；装卸时间记录
lead time 提前期
lead time offset 提前期偏置
leakage-proof 防漏
lean logistics 精益物流
lean production 精益生产
least slack per operation 最小单个工序平均时差
leg (of a voyage) 航段
length overall (overall length，简称 LOA) (船舶)总长
less container load (LCL) 拼箱货
less than container load (LCL) 拼箱货
less-than-truckload (LTL) 零担货物
letter of indemnity 担保书(函)
liable to tip 易于翻倒
lien 留置权
lift-on lift-off (LO-LO) 吊上吊下
light displacement 轻排水量
lighter 驳船
limitation of liability 责任限制
line (shipping line) 航运公司
line-haul 长途运输，干线运输
liner (liner ship) 班轮
liner in free out (LIFO) 运费不包括卸货费
liner terms 班轮条件
liner transport 班轮运输
live pilot 应用模拟
Lloyd's Register of Shipping 劳埃德船级社
load (loaded)displacement 满载排水量
loading and unloading 装卸

Appendix: Logistics Vocabularies
物流词汇

loading hatch 装货口
loading list 装货清单
loadline (load line) 载重线
log abstract 航海日志摘录
log book 航行日志
logistics 物流，后勤保证体系
logistics activity 物流活动
logistics alliance 物流联盟
logistics centre 物流中心
logistics cost 物流成本
logistics cost control 物流成本管理
logistics documents 物流单证
logistics enterprise 物流企业
logistics industry 物流产业
logistics modulus 物流模数
logistics network 物流网络
logistics operation 物流作业
logistics resource planning (LRP)物流资源计划
logistics strategy 物流战略
logistics strategy management 物流战略管理
long form B/L 全式提单
long length additional 超长附加费
long ton 长吨
longitude 经度
lot-for-lot 因需定量法
lot size 进货批量
lot size inventory 批量库存
lot sizing 批量规则
low density cargo 轻货
low-lever code 低层码
lubricating system 润滑系
lump sum charter 整笔运费租赁
lump-sum freight 整船包价运费

M

maiden voyage 处女航
main deck 主甲板
main port 主要港口
maintenance, repair, and operation supplies 维护修理操作物料
management accounting 管理会计
management by exception 例外管理法
manifest 舱单
manufacturing BOM 制造物料清单
manufacturing resource planning (MRPⅡ)制造资源计划
material requirements planning (MRPⅠ)物料需求计划
marginal cost 边际成本
maritime declaration of health 航海健康申明书
maritime lien 海事优先权
marks and numbers 唛头
master air waybill (MAWB) 航空主运单
master scheduler 主生产计划员
material available 物料可用量
material management 物料管理
material manager 物料经理
material review board 物料核定机构
mate's receipt 大副收据，收货单
maximum freight 最高运费
mean draught 平均吃水
measurement cargo 体积货物
measurement rated cargo 按体积计费的货物
measurement rules 计量规则
measure of velocity 生产速率水平
merchant (班轮提单)货方
merchant haulage 货方拖运
merchant marine 商船
MES (manufacturing executive system) 制造执行系统

metric ton 公吨
military logistics 军事物流
minimum balance 最小库存余量
minimum freight 最低运费
MIS (management information system) 管理信息系统
misdelivery 错误交货
misdescription 错误陈述
mixed cargo 混杂货
mobile crane 移动式起重机
modern materials handling 现代物料搬运
modular BOM 模块化物料单
more frequent, smaller shipments 高频次、小批量送货
more or less (MOL) 增减
more or less in charterer's option (MOLCHOP) 承租人有增减选择权
more or less in owner's option (MOLOO) 船东有增减选择权
move time 传送时间
mother ship 母船
motion and time study 动作与时间研究
MPS (master production schedule) 主生产计划
MTO (make-to-order) 订货生产
multideck ship 多层甲板船
multi-modal (inter-modal, combined) transport B/L 多式联运提单
multi-purpose cargo ship 多用途船
multi-purpose terminal 多用途场站

N

named B/L 记名提单
narrow the laycan 缩短销约期
net change 净改变法
net registered tonnage (NRT) 注册(容积)净吨
net requirements 净需求
netting 净需求计算
net weight 净重

neutral packing 中性包装

New Jason clause 新杰森条款

New York produce exchange charter-party (NYPE) 纽约土产交易所制定的定期租船合同格式

newbuilding 新船

Nippon Kaiji Kyokai (NKK) 日本船级社

no cure no pay 无效果无报酬

no customs valuation (NCV) 无声明价值

no value declared (NVD) 不要求声明价值

nominate a ship 指定船舶进行航行

non-conference line (independent line, outsider) 非公会成员的航运公司

non-delivery 未交货

non-negotiable bill of lading 不可流通的提单

non-reversible laytime 不可调配使用的装卸时间

non-vessel owning(operating) common carrier (NVOCC) 无船承运人

not always afloat but safe aground 不保持浮泊但安全搁浅

not otherwise enumerated (N.O.E.) 不另列举

note protest 作海事声明

notice of readiness (NOR) 船舶准备就绪通知书

notice of redelivery 还船通知书

notify party 通知方

not to be tripped 勿倾倒

O

ocean (liner, sea) waybill 海运单

off hire 停租

oil tanker 油轮

on board (shipped) B/L 已装船提单

on deck B/L 甲板货提单

on-carriage 货运中转

on-carrier 接运承运人

one-way pallet 单边槽货盘

open hatch bulk carrier 敞舱口散货船

open here 由此开启
open order 未结订单
open rate 优惠费率
open rated cargo 优惠费率货物
open side container 侧开式集装箱
open top container 开顶集装箱
operate a ship 经营船舶
optical character recognition 光学文字识别
option 可选件
optional cargo 选港货物
OPTO (optimized production technology) 优化生产技术
order B/L 指示提单
order cycle 订货周期
order cycle time 订货处理周期
ordering cost 订货费
order picking 拣选
order point system 订货点法
order policy 订货策略
ore/bulk/oil carrier 矿石/散货/油轮
organic peroxide 有机氧化物
out of gauge 超标(货物)
outport 小港
outsourcing 业务外包(外协，外购)
outturn 卸货
outturn report 卸货报告
outward 出港的
outward cargo 出港货
overhead apportionment/allocation 间接费分配
overhead rate, burden factor, absorption rate 间接费率
over weight surcharge 超重附加费
overweight cargo 超重货物
overlanded cargo/overlanding 溢卸货
overload 超载
overstow 堆码

overtime (O/T) 加班时间
overtonnaging 吨位过剩
owner's agents 船东代理人
oxidizing agent 氧化剂

P

package/packaging 包装
package limitation 单位(赔偿)责任限制
packing list 装箱单
packing of nominated brand 定牌包装
pallet 托(货)盘
palletized 托盘化的
pallet truck 托盘车
panamax 巴拿马型船
paramount clause 首要条款
parcel 一包，一票货
parent item 母件
Pareto Principle 帕累托原理
pegging 追溯
per freight ton (P.F.T.) 每运费吨
performance claim 性能索赔
performance measurement 业绩评价
perishable goods 易腐货物
perishable items 易腐烂的东西
permanent dunnage 固定垫舱物
PERT (program evaluation research technology) 计划评审技术
phantom 虚拟件
phosphoric acid carrier 磷酸船
product distribution 产品配送
piece weight 单重
pier 突码头
pier to pier 码头至码头运输
piggy back 驮背式运输

pilferage 偷窃
pilot 引航员
pilotage 引航
pilotage dues 引航费
place utility 空间效用
planned order releases 计划投入量
planned capacity 计划能力
planned order 计划订单
planned order receipts 计划产出量
planning BOM 计划物料单
planning horizon 计划期
platform 平台
platform flat 平台式集装箱
point of sale(POS) 销售实点(信息)系统
point of use 使用点
poison 毒剂(有毒品)
poison gas 毒气
policy and procedure 工作准则与工作规程
polythene 聚乙烯
pooling (班轮公司间分摊货物或运费)分摊制
POQ (period order quantity) 周期定货量法
port 港口，船的左舷
port congestion surcharge 港口拥挤附加费
port of refuge 避难港
port surcharge 港口附加费
portable unloader 便携式卸货机
possession utility 所有权效用
post fixture 订约后期工作
post-entry 追补报关单
power assisting device 助力装置
power supply device 供能装置
power train 传动系
priority 优先级
preamble (租船合同)前言

pre-entry 预报单
pre-shipment charges 运输前费用
pre-stow 预定积载
private carrier 私人承运人
private form 自用式租船合同
production logistics 生产物流
proforma charter-party 租约格式
produce carrier 侧开式集装箱
product (products) carrier 液体货运输船
projected available balance 预计可用库存量
promotional rate 促销费率
production activity control 生产作业控制
production cycle 生产周期
propeller shaft 传动轴
proposed cost 建议成本
prospects 预期
prototyping, computer pilot 原型测试
protecting (protective, supervisory) agent 船东利益保护人
protection and indemnity club (association) (P.& I. Club, Pandi Club) 船东保赔协会
protective clauses 保护性条款
protest 海事声明
PTF (planned time fence) 计划时界
pumpman 泵工
put away 存储
purchase (吊杆)滑车组

Q

quantity gross 毛需求量
quantity allocation 已分配量
quarter ramp 船尾跳板
quarter-deck 后甲板
quay 码头
queue time 排队时间
quick response (QR) 快速反应

quote 报价

R

radioactive 放射性物品
radio frequency (RF) 无线射频
railcar 有轨车
railway container yard 铁路集装箱场
ramp 跳板
ramp/hatch cover (跳板)舱口盖
rate 费率
rated capacity 额定能力
rate of demurrage 滞期费率
rate of discharge (discharging) 卸货率
rate of freight 运费率
rate of loading 装货速率
RCCP (rough-cut capacity planning) 粗能力计划
received for shipment B/L 备运(收妥待运)提单
receiving dates 收货期间
receiving space 收货区
recharter 转租
recovery agent 追偿代理
redelivery (redly) 还船
redelivery certificate 还船证书
refrigerated (reefer) ship 冷藏船
refrigerated (reefer)container 冷藏集装箱
regeneration 全重排法
register 登记，报到
register (registered) tonnage 登记吨位
registration 登记，报到
Registro Italiano Navale (R.I.) 意大利船级社
release a bill of lading 交提单
release cargo 放货
released order, open order 下达订单

remaining on board (R.O.B.) 船上所有
removable deck 活动甲板
repetitive manufacturing 重复式生产
reporting point (calling-in-point) 报告点
reposition containers 调配集装箱
requisition 请购单
required capacity 需用能力
resource requirements planning 资源需求计划
respondentia loan 船货抵押贷款
resupply order 补库单
return cargo 回程货
return load 回程装载
return trip C/P 往返航次租船合同
reversible laytime 可调配的装卸时间
roads (roadstead) 港外锚地
rolling cargo 滚装货物
rolling hatch cover 滚动舱单
roll-on roll-off (RO-RO) 滚上滚下
roll-on roll-off ship 滚装船
rotation 港序
round the world (service) (R.T.W.) 全球性服务
round voyage 往返航次
routing 工艺路线
run aground 搁浅
running days 连续日
running gear 行驶系
run time 加工时间

S

safe berth (S.B.) 安全泊位
safe port (S.P.) 安全港口
safe aground 安全搁浅
safe working load 安全工作负荷

Appendix: Logistics Vocabularies
物流词汇

safety lead time 安全提前期
safety radio-telegraphy certificate 无线电报设备安全证书
safety stock 安全库存
said to contain (S.T.C.) (提单术语)内货据称
sail 航行，离港
sailing schedule (card) 船期表
sales package 销售包装
salvage agreement 救助协议
salvage charges 救助费
salve 救助
salvor 救助人
Saturdays, Sundays and holidays excepted (S.S.H.E.X.) 星期六、日与节假日除外
Saturdays, Sundays and holidays included (S.S.H.I.N.C) 星期六、日与节假日包括在内
SCANCON 斯堪人航次租船合同
Scanconbill 斯堪人航次租船合同提单
scantlings 构件尺寸
scheduler 计划员
scheduled airline 班机运输
scheduled receipts 计划接收量
scrap 废品率
scrap terminal 废料场
seasonal stock 季节储备
sea waybill 海运提单
seal 密封
seaworthiness 船舶适航
secure (to) 固定
segregated ballast tank 分隔压载水舱
self-sustaining ship 自备起重机的集装箱船
self-trimming ship (self-trimmer) 自动平舱船
self-unloader 自卸船
semi-container ship 半集装箱船
semitrailer 半挂车(在后部有一套或若干套轮子，前部由牵引车或牵引机动车支撑的挂车)
separation 隔票
service contract 服务合同

set-up time 准备时间
shakeproof 防震
shears (shear-legs) 人字(起重)架
sheave 滑轮
shelf life 保存期
shelter-deck 遮蔽甲板船
shift 工班
shift (to) 移泊，移位
shifting charges 移泊费
shipbroker 船舶经纪人
shipment 装运的货物
shipper 托运人，发货人
shipping 航运，船舶，装运
shipping agency 船务代理
shipping by chartering 租船运输
shipping instructions 装运须知
shipping line 航运公司
shipping order (S/O) 装货单 (下货纸)
shipping space 发货区
ship's gear 船上起重设备
ship's rail 船舷
ship's tackle 船用索具
ship-to 交货地
ship to ship transfer 过驳
shipyard 造船厂
shop calendar 工厂日历
shop floor control 车间作业控制
shop order 车间订单
shore 货撑
shore gear 岸上设备(岸吊)
short form B/L 简式提单
short sea 近海
short shipment 短装
shortage 短少

Appendix: Logistics Vocabularies
物流词汇

shortlanded cargo 短卸货物
shrinkage 缩减率
shut out (to) 短装
side door container 侧门集装箱
side-loading trailer 侧向装卸拖车
similar substitute (sim.sub.) 相似替换船
simulated cost 模拟成本
single deck ship (S.D.) 单层甲板船
single hatch ship 单舱船
single trip C/P 单航次租船合同
sister ship 姐妹船
skid 垫木
skip 吊货盘
sliding hatch cover 滑动舱盖
sling 吊货索(链)环,吊起
slop tank 污水箱
slops 污水
slot 箱位
SMED (single-minute exchange of dies) 快速换模法
societal logistics 社会物流
SOP (sales and operations planning) 销售与动作规划
sorting 分拣
sound-proof 隔音
space utilization 空间利用率
special commodity quotation (SCQ) 特种商品报价
special equipment 特殊设备
specific cargo container 特种货物集装箱
specific commodity rates (SCR) 特种货物运价
specific gravity(S.G.) 比重
spending variance, expenditure variance 开支差异
spiral elevator 螺旋式卸货机
spontaneously combustible 自燃物品
spreader 横撑(集装箱吊具)
squat 船身下沉

stacking 堆码
stacking crane 堆垛机
stale B/L 过期提单
standard cost system 标准成本体系
starboard (side) 右舷
statement of facts 事实记录
starting system 起动系
steering gear 转向器
steering linkage 转向传动装置
steering system 转向系
steering wheel 转向盘
stem 船艏，装期供货
stem a berth 预订泊位
stereoscopic warehouse 立体仓库
stern 船尾
stevedore 装卸工人
stevedoring charges 装卸费用
stevedore's (docker's, hand) hook 手钩
stiff 稳性过大
stocktaking 盘点
storage 保管
storage duration 存储期
storehouse 库房
storing 储存
stowage factor 积载因素(系数)
stowage plan 货物积载计划
stranding 搁浅
strengthened hold 加固舱
strike clause 罢工条款
strike-bound 罢工阻碍
strip (destuff) a container 卸集装箱
strip seal 封条
stuff (to) 装集装箱
sub-charterer 转租人

sub-freight 转租运费
subject (sub.) details 有待协商的细节
subject (sub.) stem 装期供货待定
subject free (open) 待定条款
subrogation 代位追偿权
substitue 替代船，替换
substitution 换船
suit time 起诉期
summarized BOM 汇总物料清单
summer draught 夏季吃水
summer freeboard 夏季干舷
suspension 悬架
supply chain 供应链
supply chain management(SCM) 供应链管理
supply chian integration 供应链整合
support ship 辅助船
synchronous manufacturing 同步制造

T

tackle 索具(滑车)
tally 理货
tally clerk 理货员
tally sheet (book) 理货单
tank car 槽车
tank cleaning 油舱清洗
tank container 液体集装箱
tank terminal (farm) 油罐场
tanker 油轮
tariff 费率表
tarpaulin 油布
tear off here 由此撕开
temperature limit 温度极限
tender 稳性过小

terminal chassis 场站拖车
terminal handling charge 场站操作费
temperature controlled space 温度可控区
third-party logistics (TPL) 第三方物流
through B/L 联运提单
throughput 吞吐量
through traffic 联运
through transport 直达运输
through rate 联运费率
tier limit (limitation) 层数限制
time bar 时效丧失
time bucket 时段
time charter 期租
time charter party 定期租船合同
time-critical shelf lives 短的保质期
time sheet 装卸时间表
time fence 时界
time zone 时区
time utility 时间效用
TOC (theory of constraints) 约束理论
to be nominated (TBN) 指定船舶
tolerated outsider 特许非会员公司
tomming (down) 撑货
tones per centimeter (TPC) 每厘米吃水吨数
tones per day (TPD) 每天装卸吨数
tones per inch (TPI) 每英寸吃水吨数
total lead time 总提前期
top management commitment 领导承诺
top stow cargo 堆顶货
total deadweight (TDW) 总载重量
tracer (货物)查询单
tractor 牵引车
trade blocks 贸易壁垒
trading limits 航行范围

Appendix: Logistics Vocabularies
物流词汇

trailer 拖车
tramp transport 不定期(租船)运输
transfer (equipment handover) charge 设备租用费
transfer device 传动装置
transfer transport 中转运输
transshipment (trans-shipment) 转船
transit cargo 过境货物
transit time 传送时间
transportation inventory, pipeline stock 在途库存
transporter crane 轨道式起重机
transport package 运输包装
transship (trans-ship) 转船
transshipment B/L 转船提单
tray 货盘
trim 平舱
trim a ship 调整船舶吃水
truckload (TL) 一货车的容量
tug 拖轮
turn round (around, or turnaround) time 船舶周转时间
turn time 等泊时间
tween deck 二层甲板
twenty equivalent unit (TEU) 二十尺集装箱换算单位
twin hatch vessel 双舱口船
two-way pallet 两边开槽托盘

U

ultra large crude carrier (ULCC) 超大型油轮
unclean (foul, dirty) B/L 不清洁提单
uncontainerable (uncontainerisable) cargo 不适箱货
under deck shipment 货舱运输
unit load 成组运输
unit loading and unloading 单元装卸
unit load devices (ULD) 集装设备

unitisation 成组化

universal bulk carrier (UBC) 通用散装货船

unload 卸货

unmoor 解揽

unseaworthiness 不适航

upward 向上，由下往上

use no hooks 请勿倒挂，禁止手钩

utilization 整箱货

V

valuation charges 声明价值费

valuation form 货价单

valuation scale 货价表

value-added logistics service 增值物流服务

value-added network 增值网

value-added chain 增值链

value chain 价值链

valve timing mechanism 配气机构

vehicle /train ferry 汽车/火车渡轮

vendor managed inventory (VMI) 供应商管理库存

ventilated container 通风集装箱

ventilation 通风

ventilator 通风器

vessel 船舶，船方

vessel sharing agreement (V.S.A.) 船舶共用协议

virtual logistics 虚拟物流

virtual organization 虚拟企业

virtual warehouse 虚拟仓库

void filler 填充物

volume variance 产量差异

voyage (trip) charter 航次租船

voyage account 航次报表

voyage charter party 航次租船合同

voyage charter party on time basis 航次期租合同

W

wait time 等待时间
warehouse 仓库
warning mark 警告性标志
warehouse layout 仓库布局
warehouse management system (WMS) 仓库管理系统
waste material logistics 废弃物物流
water-proof 防水
waybill 货运单
weather permitting (W.P.) 天气允许
weather working days (W.W.D.) 良好天气工作日
weather-bound 天气阻挠
weight cargo 重量货
weight or measure (measurement) (W/M) 重量/体积
weight rated cargo 计重货物
well 货井，井区
wharf 码头
wharfage (charges) 码头费
wheel 车轮
when where ready on completion of discharge (W.W.R.C.D.) 何时何处还船
whether in berth or not (W.I.B.O.N.) 无论靠泊与否
whether in free pratique or not (W.I.F.P.O.N.) 无论是否通过检验
whether in port or not (W.I.P.O.N.) 不论是否在港内
white (clean, clean petroleum) products 精炼油
wide laycan 长销约期
with effect from (W.E.F.) 自生效
workable (working) hatch 可工作舱口
working day 工作日
working day of 24 consecutive hours 连续 24 小时工作日
working day of 24 hours 24 小时工作日
working time saved (W.T.S.) 节省的装卸时间
work-in-process inventory 在制品库存

work center 工作中心
work flow 工作流
work order 车间订单

Y

yard (shipyard) 造船厂

Z

zero inventory 零库存

References 参考文献

[1] Alan Rushion, John Oxley, Phil Croucher. The Handbook of Logistics and Distribution Management [M]. Atomic Dog Publishing, 2002.

[2] Managing International Logistics [M]. International Trade Centre UNCTAD/WTO, 2000.

[3] Martin Christopher. Logsitics and Supply Chain Management: Strategies for Reducing Cost and Improving Service [M]. 2nd ed. Financial Times Prentice Hall, 2003.

[4] Paul R. Murphy, Donald F.Wood. Contemporary Logistics [M]. New York Pearson Prentice Hall Business Publishing, 2004.

[5] Pierre David, Richard Stewart. International Logistics—the Management of International Trade Operations [M]. 2nd ed. Beijing: Tsinghua University Press, 2007.

[6] Susan Lau，黎凡，毛立群. 物流英语[M]. 上海：上海外语教育出版社，2009.

[7] 白世贞. 物流英语[M]. 北京：中国物资出版社，2004.

[8] 陈明新. 商务英语常用文书100例[M]. 大连：大连理工大学出版社，2007.

[9] 对外经济贸易大学国际经贸学院运输系. 国际货物运输实务[M]. 北京：对外经济贸易大学出版社，1999.

[10] 李珍. 物流英语[M]. 厦门：厦门大学出版社，2011.

[11] 李彦萍. 实用物流英语[M]. 北京：对外经济贸易大学出版社，2007.

[12] 李婉冰. 物流商务英语实用手册[M]. 北京：中国纺织出版社，2007.

[13] 乐美龙. 现代物流英语[M]. 上海：上海交通大学出版社，2007.

[14] 牛国崎. 物流专业英语[M]. 北京：北京理工大学出版社，2007.

[15] 刘浩. 物流专业实用英语[M]. 武汉：华中科技大学出版社，2009.

[16] 上海对外贸易协会. 进出口单证实务[M]. 北京：中国对外经济贸易出版社，1995.

[17] 石本俊. 商贸英语[M]. 广州：广东旅游出版社，2007.

[18] 童宏祥. 外贸跟单实务[M]. 上海：上海财经大学出版社，2006.

[19] 王传见. 国际货代物流实务英语手册[M]. 上海：华东理工大学出版社，2004.

[20] 王芬. 实用外贸英语函电[M]. 北京：中国商业出版社，2004.

[21] 吴健，黄金万，傅莉萍. 现代物流专业英语[M]. 北京：机械工业出版社，2009.

[22] 闫静雅. 物流专业英语[M]. 北京：机械工业出版社，2007.

[23] 杨丽华，董俊英，刘燕一. 贸易实务英语[M]. 北京：首都经济贸易大学出版社，2006.

[24] 杨性如，万笑影. 物流英语[M]. 上海：上海科学技术文献出版社，2003.

[25] 杨瑛. 物流英语口语教程[M]. 天津：南开大学出版社，2004.

[26] 周宁，王智利. 物流英语[M]. 北京：电子工业出版社，2011.

[27] 仲颖,尹新. 物流专业英语[M]. 北京:中国农业大学出版社,2011.

[28] 郑润萍. 国际物流实用英语[M]. 北京:中国物资出版社,2009.

[29] http://www.wisegeek.com/what-is-edi.html

[30] http://www.chinaknowledge.com

[31] http://www.packworld.com